WHAT HAPPENS BEFORE WE ARE BORN

Also by Arie Boogert from Lindisfarne Books

What Happens after We Die: Making the Connection between the Living and the Dead

WHAT HAPPENS BEFORE WE ARE BORN

Creating Our Living Web of Destiny

ARIE BOOGERT

with prayers and meditations by Rudolf Steiner

Lindisfarne Books | 2021

Lindisfarne Books
An imprint of SteinerBooks / Anthroposophic Press, Inc.
402 Union Street, No. 58, Hudson, NY 12534
www.steinerbooks.org

 Originally published in Dutch as *Ons Voorland: Rudolf Steiner over het leven na dit leven* (Uitgeverij Christofoor, Zeist, Netherlands, 2000).

Translated by Philip Mees
Book design by Jens Jensen

Bible quotations are from New International Version (Old Testament) and Jon Madsen, *The New Testament: A Rendering.*

Library of Congress Control Number: 9781584209133
ISBN: 978-1-58420-913-3 (paperback)
ISBN: 978-1-58420-914-0 (ebook)

Contents

Introduction: Exploring the Hereafter

"Life after life" has been a subject of increasing interest in the past several decades, to such an extent that it has given rise to a kind of subculture. Experiences on the boundary of life and death have become widely known through the books of Elisabeth Kübler-Ross, Raymond Moody, and many others. People everywhere have come to feel that after death we might not be so totally dead as was generally believed a few decades ago, but when we ask what life after death is really like, most voices fall silent.

Recently I found the book *After Death: Mapping the Journey* by Sukie Miller, a psychotherapist who researched what happens to us after death. In the book, she tackles the problem seriously, and she even established an institute to study the hereafter. She investigates all sorts of cultures and people, ordering her material and finding some typical stages in "life after life" that are interesting to consider; we will encounter these in the course of this volume. Her book is intended to help readers "map" the journey that awaits all of us.

One distinctive element in Miller's book is her "postmortem inventory," a list with 159 propositions, arranged according to seven themes. We are to become conscious of what we think of the hereafter—our mental pictures and beliefs related to it. We are asked to check everything that speaks to us, as well as our degree of conviction. Then we write down our answers to indicate the degree to which a proposition appeals to us.

Rudolf Steiner occupies a single paragraph in her book, appearing as one of three "visionary travelers" who relate the nature of the journey through the realms on the other side of death. Dr. Miller arrived at this approach based on lectures by Steiner in 1912 and 1913. During those years, he explained the journey of the soul after death through the planetary spheres, an aspect I will discuss in chapter 6.* In this description we find an example of the way he familiarized his listeners with death and all that follows until a new birth.

We would have to study a large number of Rudolf Steiner's collected works to get a complete impression of what he said on the subject. In his books, and especially in his thousands of lectures, the subjects of death, life after death, the way the dead go through the world of spirit, and karma and reincarnation all turn up with astonishing frequency. In his descriptions, Steiner repeatedly gave an impression of the view he chose for a given occasion. Each time, he seems to have had a clear perception of the questions that lived in his listeners.

Why did Rudolf Steiner work this way? One reason is certainly his experience that we have to radically take our way of thinking, all of our inner attitudes and images, back to the drawing board if we want to enter the realm of life after this life. If we want to create a "map" of that realm, it will have to be our most individualized kind of map—indeed, our very own individual map. If we tried to put everything on one map to create harmony (as occurred, for example, in the Gospels) we would have to gloss over all the particulars for the sake of a coherent story. This is why I want to place some of Steiner's

* Rudolf Steiner, *Life between Death and Rebirth;* and *Between Death and Rebirth* (please see the bibliography for details on this and other cited works).

descriptions side-by-side in this book, and in this way make a series of smaller maps, as it were, of several exploratory trips. I try to give the reader an impression of what awaits us.

It depends completely on us how we enter that realm and exactly where we step into it. That realm exists as a domain of life and constant change, so that the impressions we gain and our experiences there depend on us. Perhaps it is initially most comparable with experiences in the world of dreams. Can we escape being swept along? How do we keep our footing there? How do we preserve our identity? Such are the questions that arise as we begin to prepare for the journey that will take us into the realm of death, which we could well call "our future homeland."

Before I say more about "our future homeland," I want to emphasize that, for Rudolf Steiner, life after life exists by the grace of reincarnation and karma. We do not simply die; the life after life that we begin after dying gradually transforms into "life before life." It leads to a new embodiment, a new birth. First of all, a settling of destiny awaits us after death based on our karma—the consequences of the totality of our deeds and lack of deeds during the life just ended. To a large extent, this settling of destiny determines the particulars for the beginning of the life journey that follows the end of our earthly life.

Dealing with Death and Dying

In my book *What Happens after We Die,* I take the reader through the experiences of the deceased in the first three days after dying; and we also considered the burial or cremation that follow these. We used prayers and meditative verses to follow our deceased on their way into the world of spirit. In that book I wanted to give an impression of what Rudolf Steiner said on the subject of dealing with death and dying and with the first experiences following death.

Toward the end of *What Happens after We Die,* I gave a short list of what I had not described—namely, the journey of the soul after death through the worlds of soul and spirit and the way we live outside the earthly body with our soul forces after we die. I also did not discuss the ways in which the dead are active in the world of the living, nor the way destiny is formed and transformed from one life to the next.

In this volume, I take the reader into a realm that is, in the most encompassing form, our future homeland and, following what Rudolf Steiner had to say about it, again juxtapose many of his descriptions to create an impression of what awaits us.

For an effort such as this, we should use experiences that do not depend so much on the person of the deceased. Such experiences do not need to be less concrete because the world of our deceased is part of the world that surrounds us every day. Nevertheless, it is a completely different reality. Normally, we pay no attention to that world and our experiences with it; we never notice how the world of those who have died is present in our own world. We have to begin to observe and interpret; we have to train ourselves somewhat to become aware of what is so obviously present in our lives and in our world, though initially unnoticed completely. We have to learn to "see"; to do this we have to assemble the necessary concepts and mental images of such a completely different world and existence.

People who have read and critiqued *What Happens after We Die* said, among other things, that it is too repetitive and has too many references. It seems to me that this is necessary for the approach I am using. It was not my objective merely to convey facts and a lot of abstract knowledge about dying and death. Rather, I wanted to introduce a dimension that directly touches everyone who has just lost a loved person. We can then take a book such as *What Happens after We Die* and look for a chapter that speaks to us. We don't go into the subject in an abstract way; we are directly involved with it. Maybe then we want to read on, or leaf through the book and pick a different chapter. We may notice how our inner expectations change as we become familiar with what the deceased are experiencing. We will feel a need to stop and reflect and check our feelings. Repetition and references might be helpful when the point is not to gain knowledge through discourse, but to learn how to deal with something, to learn to live with it.

With *What Happens before We Are Born,* we are trying to penetrate the realm (or should we say sphere, dimension, domain?) where those who have died live; it asks of us again to break through our habitual patterns of thinking. This happens when, in the words of John the Baptist, we begin to change our hearts and minds (Matt. 3:2). The Baptist called for people to do this, because he perceived how "the realm of the heavens" had come near. The Godhead and the powers of heaven are much more directly present in this realm than usually here on Earth, and it is the sphere in which the dead live. After death we begin to penetrate that realm.

Surrounding the body of the deceased on the deathbed, this very different reality is almost palpably present. It increases our shyness as we approach the deceased. We sense how we have to change our whole way of thinking, for only then can we understand something about the realm opened by death.

In our time, Rudolf Steiner's Anthroposophy is one great effort to help people to come to such a change of worldview and thinking. Steiner always tried, through his use of words, not only to give us a glimpse of that very different reality, but also to evoke it for us. For example, when he described how human beings go their way into death, he used several concepts that we will explore.

In this introduction, I want to contemplate the four primary members of our being, and in doing so I will use words I cannot explain further without expanding this introduction into an entire book. The etheric world, elemental world, kamaloka, the actual spiritual world, and the heavenly hierarchies—for now, simply accept them as given. They will all be discussed further in following chapters.

Life after This Life

When we die, we leave our body behind—the *physical body*, the dead material body, or corpse. It is the dust that begins to return to dust (Gen. 3:19). Yet, what we see there is not the complete physical body but only the part of it that comes from the Earth, the body in its material form.

The physical body also has an invisible, suprasensory part, which we may call the "form body"; it gives form to the body and maintains that form throughout earthly life (see appendix 1, pp. 209-211). This suprasensory part of the body cannot die, but separates at death from the "dust" of the physical body to go its own way; it becomes suprasensory and spiritual again. It once again becomes part of the universe that surrounds the Earth, planets, and fixed stars. Part of this suprasensory physical body, however, remains connected with the Earth—the part that lives in warmth. Once death has definitively broken the unity of the physical body, we plunge with the rest of it—quickly as lightning—into the spiritual formative forces that are the basis of our physical body. In the realm formed by these formative forces, having become infinitely large and broad, we live between death and a subsequent birth.

What lies on the deathbed is therefore merely the part of the physical body with which we ever more increasingly identified after birth. Along with the form body, which has found its place in the cosmos, we return to the archetypal image of the macrocosmic human being that formed itself into a human figure "in the beginning."

Once we come to realize all of this, we face one of the processes that show us how "different" spiritual reality is. Each time we are born, the Earth makes the material part of the physical body available to us. What gives form to the body gathers into it from the widths of the cosmos. The forces that form our human form are much older than all that, in our terms, is earthly, physical, or material, and are thus also far more spiritual.

To enable this form to connect itself to the Earth, however, it must be "turned" inside out, just as a glove can be turned inside out. We are all turned inside out—in other words, viewed spiritually our inside during life (stomach, intestines, and various other organs) becomes our outside. It becomes the outer, although it is still unfinished and is only beginning its cosmic development. The senses through which we interact with this physical world and form our exterior during earthly life are actually much more inner than the "spiritual outside" we carry within us.

We can thus try to familiarize ourselves with the idea that our exterior is much more inner than our interior (our *spatial* interior) is, whereas the latter becomes much more outer than our earthly exterior is. We will return to the spiritual law, or principle, of turning inside out.

Now that we have considered the twofold nature of our physical, material body and the form body, we can take the next step. In biblical terms, the form body is the body in which the resurrected Christ appeared to his disciples—the "Resurrection body." Living in this body, He is no longer hindered by closed doors or distances (see appendices 1 and 2).

Living Web of Destiny

We can observe something in the body of the deceased other than the material substance beginning to return to dust. We realize first that there are still remnants of life in the dead body—for example, in the hair and nails, which continue to grow for a while. These remnants of the life that made the body grow also disappear once decomposition of the abandoned physical body is under way.

What we can still observe in those few days are the traces of the etheric, or life, body. During life it not only maintains our body, it is also the bearer of our memory. During the first three or four days after death, memories of the deceased arise for them as a great tableau, or panorama of life. So long as this tableau lasts, the connection between the etheric and physical bodies is not entirely broken.

The etheric body, or life body, is our first suprasensory body and invisible to physical eyes. During the days when we can stand by the deathbed with the body of the deceased, the etheric body is in the process of withdrawing from its connection to the physical body. What was the nature of this connection? Let's imagine a porous earthenware pot filled with liquid; that liquid will disappear completely into the porous stoneware. The etheric body is similarly connected with the physical body during life; it is completely absorbed into it.

After death, when the etheric body begins to loosen itself from the physical body, it begins to grow in size and spread into the cosmos, the sphere of the etheric. Viewed from Earth, this is a process of "dissolving," just as sugar dissolves into water; once dissolved, however it remains demonstrably present. Likewise, the individual etheric body maintains an individual existence in the etheric world when it connects with it, and then it imprints into it the experiences the deceased during earthly life.

Viewed spiritually, the etheric body is absorbed into the etheric world. Rudolf Steiner used the German word *Inbindung* for this, meaning "integrating," in contrast to "disintegrating."* As the dead physical body goes through a process of disintegration, the etheric body is integrated (without losing its individual existence). With the expansion of the etheric body, our spiritual consciousness also grows as we watch the fruit of our life go into the widths of space.

Like any spiritual event, this process is not "anonymous"; it is not something that just happens. The human web of destiny in the etheric body that separates from the material body is taken up by the spiritual beings nearest to the human being, the *Angels* of the third heavenly hierarchy, which consists of the spiritual beings closest to us as human beings. These are the "angels," a name given to all the spiritual beings who have ever revealed themselves to human beings, including the *Archangels* and the primal powers, the *Archai*. They breathe in the web woven by human destiny and receive it into themselves.

Part of the etheric body, however—a kind of extract or summary of the life panorama of the deceased during the first days after death—stays with the individuality on the way into the worlds of spirit. It serves as support for the astral body and forms a kind of "skeleton" that, in a concentrated form, preserves the memories of events during one's life.

* Rudolf Steiner, *Chance, Providence, and Necessity*, p. 123.

The Moral Human Being

The longer we stand by the body of a deceased person we have known, the more strongly memories will arise in us about the person whose face we see before us. In addition to memories of all kinds of incidents in life, impressions of the individuality will arise that showed itself to us from many different sides. This individuality lives on after death in two purely suprasensory members of his being that, when the person was dying, separate immediately from the dead body—immediately and absolutely, not gradually as the etheric body does. With Rudolf Steiner, we use the terms *astral body* and *"I"*; neither can be seen by the physical eye, but we clearly experience their presence.

When these suprasensory members have separated themselves from the earthly body, the deceased come to consciousness of themselves again. On Earth we human beings need the body in order to come to self-consciousness; thanks to the death of that body we arrive at consciousness of ourselves in the world of spirit. Even while people are still standing by the deathbed the deceased begin to come to themselves in the retrospective of the moment of dying. As they thus look at themselves in death from the outside, one could say, the deceased find their "I"-consciousness again.

The first of these two suprasensory members is the astral body, our human "star body." Whereas the material body belongs to the Earth and the etheric body to an elemental world that surrounds the Earth cosmically, our "star body" is at home in the world of the planets and fixed stars. During our life on Earth, the astral body and "I" use the earthly unity of physical and etheric bodies as their dwelling by day. During sleep they dwell in the spiritual world that underlies our outer, sensory world. With the aid of our etheric and material corporeality, into which we return when we awake from sleep, we are in contact by day with the sensory world itself. When dying, however, we enter another spiritual world—namely the one we left at birth. According to Steiner, one spiritual world generates the sensory world; the other generates us human beings.

For some time after death, the astral body preserves the earthly identity it formed during earthly life. Then we get busy coming to terms with the life we led—all that happened or did not happen. This takes place as we go back through our life in reverse, beginning with death and ending at birth. Once we have worked through everything that binds us to the Earth, we will have freed ourselves from all earthly ties. At this point we can surrender our astral body, and the true spiritual world can open up for us; we feel how we are fully imbued inwardly with the spirit.

As the astral body becomes part of the universe, in worlds of soul and spirit, it continues to exist as such. It does not dissolve as the etheric body did but maintains its autonomy and develops further in the world of soul and spirit. Part of the astral body, however, remains behind like a piece of baggage that is checked until the owner picks it up again; this part consists of our "moral values." On our journey into the universe we leave it behind in the realm where we lived through our life again in reverse.

This "package," as it is sometimes called, contains everything that still binds the human being to earthly existence. It is like a second kind of human being—our moral being. During the first period after dying, we have this before us as a living picture. During life it was formed from the substance of the astral cosmos as a kind of spiritual, elementary being. Thus it accompanies us in the forms of its members, as a living image of our moral, spiritual being.

Once we have given up that "second" human being, the true spiritual world opens up to us. But this, too, is not an anonymous process. What the deceased experience when they live through their life again in reverse is taken up by the essential being of the angels of the second, higher heavenly hierarchy we know as the *Exousiai* (*Powers*), *Dynamis* (*Virtues*), and *Kyriotetes* (*Dominions*). In them the consequences of their life come alive and receive a spiritual right of existence, they become reality.

What We Call Our "I"

Like the astral body, the human "I" cannot be physically perceived, but it can be experienced. However, here we need to be careful. The "I" we recognize in one another is merely a reflection of our true "I" in the physical body. When we are born, the true "I" and astral body remain behind in the world of spirit; they do not enter physical existence. The etheric body acts as the mediator between the physical body and the two higher members.

At death, we leave our physical body behind and immediately submerge ourselves in the now-cosmic form body, and now we find our "I"-consciousness again in the retrospect of dying. The thought of the physical body now begins to live in the astral body and "I." The disintegration of the body into its elements will keep awareness of our physical body alive during the entire time following death. Because of our memory of the physical body we know we are an "I."

Whereas our astral body is our "star" body, the "I" has its home outside the world of stars in the domain of the divine Trinity. We are independent of the cosmos in our "I." During life our destiny works in this "I" as a kind of spiritual instinct that leads us to people and situations that give us the possibility of making something of our destiny. What we make of our destiny in our confrontations with others transcends the destiny of an individual person; it is what the angels who creatively generate everything earthly look for. It is accepted and worked through by the angels of the first, or highest, heavenly hierarchy, the *Thrones, Cherubim,* and *Seraphim.*

Here we have to realize something noteworthy about what we experience as our "everyday 'I,'" which we have to distinguish from our "true 'I,'" which remains outside the gate of birth. How do we experience this ordinary "I"? Oddly enough, it is never directly present in all that fills our life, but only indirectly in the discontinuity of our experiences—between our experiences. We perceive our "I" in the blind spots of our conscious life, where our will does not become conscious.

If our "I" lived in our consciousness we would always only be aware of our self in our social contacts and thus ignore others. Fortunately, our "I" lives in what does *not* come to consciousness, and thus we are open to the "I" of the other person. We are even too open, for the experience of the "I" of the other puts us momentarily into a condition of slight stupor, letting us doze off; we sense our own "I" again only when we start resisting this. The other asks for our attention, and in the process lets us doze off; we resist this and assert ourselves so that we can wake up in ourselves and let the other doze off in turn. Thus each encounter consists of a continuous alternation between dozing off in the other and waking up in our self. In this way we always meet each other in our ordinary "I" unconsciously. Yes, social contact would be actually impossible if we did not doze off into each other to build a bridge between each other.

Can we bring a certain level of consciousness into our encounters with others—not just in our daily interactions with one another but also in regard to the barrier posed by death? With this question in the background, we can now take up our theme: *life after earthly life.*

1

Toward the Sun

We are born at a particular moment in time and at a very particular place on Earth. The same is true when we die. Birth and death, however, are both processes that last beyond a single moment. The moment of birth shows only a snapshot, as does the moment of dying. Long before birth, we are already living toward it, and our birth continues long after we are born. Similarly, dying announces itself in a gradual physical dismantling and decline and in many kinds of phenomena of detachment. Moreover, we can distinguish phases in the processes of both birth and death. At the heart of the dying process is the moment of death.

Some phases of the dying process were mentioned briefly in the introduction, describing how the deceased cast off the members of their being one after the other. These phases of the dying process—cutting our ties to the Earth—turn out to be a mirror image of a birth process, that of being received in the world of spirit. With the poet Novalis, we discover that "the human being is born when the spirit dies, and the spirit is born when the human being dies."* Moreover, at the beginning of life we see the reflection of a spiritual dying process visibly before us as a process of birth, and at death we expect a birthing process as the reflection of the earthly dying process.

* Novalis, *Wenn ein Geist stirbt, wird er Mensch. Wenn der Mensch stirbt, wird er Geist*. Freiberger Studien, 1798–99.

The phases of this remain hidden to our daily observation; we need someone like Rudolf Steiner to clarify this for us. At one time, however, the reflection of the earthly dying process became visible—after the death on the cross on Golgotha when, to their bewilderment, people were confronted with Christ's Resurrection. The angels asked the women who were seeking the body of the Crucified One and entering the tomb, "Why do you seek the Living One among the dead? He is not here, he has risen" (Luke 24:5–6). The women had come to care for the body of the deceased person, but no body was to be found. With their question, the angels helped the women overcome their astonishment; they awakened in them an initial consciousness of resurrection, or life after dying.

We continue to sense a kind of autumn mood hanging over death—fear that, along with all that dies on Earth, it is not just the mortal human being who goes the way of all dust. The landscape of death is mostly shrouded in mist, the mists that float above the western seas into which people in ancient times saw their dead disappear. For too many of us, our dead are like annual plants that don't make it through the winter of death. People are often caught by this autumn mood on occasions such as Memorial Day, even knowing that, although we die, we are "perennials" and do not perish with death.

Before the women entered the empty tomb, the sun had risen on Golgotha. In the rays of the rising sun, they saw that the stone had been rolled away from the tomb, and they learned that the living was not to be found among the dead. This means that from our graves, too, a stone has been removed; the sun of the resurrection has risen over them. Ever since Christ rose, we are assured of a first resurrection that wakes the soul to life. We may hope for a second resurrection that will restore our form body and liberate it from the burden of physical death (see appendix 2 on the resurrection body).

"Why do you seek the living among the dead?" This is a question we need to ask ourselves time and again if we wish to accompany our dead on their way from death to a new birth and want to understand this journey. In its beginning, the journey has four phases.

The Way from Death to a New Birth

After death we retrace the way we came as we moved toward birth. We have to shake off our earthly orientation and acquire a "form" adapted to the spiritual world. The angular articulation of space in length, breadth, and height gives us our earthly orientation; the sphere with its roundness gives us our spiritual orientation. As a permanent reminder of our pre-birth existence, we carry a picture of the cosmos in our head. Is it also true that the Earth itself preserves in its form the memory of a cosmic past, though it imposes very different forms on its inhabitants?

On our way to Earth we begin to orient ourselves on straight earthly lines and angles, and the organs in the chest, especially the lungs and the heart, preserve the partially spherical form of a half-globe, which is sometimes barely recognizable. This half-sphere has, by our standards, its infinitely distant center in the East. The other organs in the lower body, as well as the limbs, already show typically earthly forms. No pre-birth influence lingers here, but our immediate and direct concern at birth already steps in—the location on the Earth's surface where our parents and ancestors primarily live. This territory gives its particular color to the forces that, radiating from the center of the Earth, fashion the embryo; the forces in Australia are different from those in Europe, and in America they are again different. Bearing evidence in our constitution of these various influences, we finally come into the world at a specific moment in time as a human being, with the special nuances provided by the forces of our earthly environment, the forces of, let's say, our "earthly cosmos."

The human being, image of the cosmos, was formed in these four phases before birth in the gradual confrontation with earthly forces and must adapt again to the cosmos after dying. This also takes place in four phases—those of detachment, integration, letting go, and being incorporated.

During the days when the etheric body is in the process of dissolving and integrating into the etheric world, the connection of the deceased with the physical body weakens. Then the influences of the planets and their constellations leave their aftereffects in the etheric body. This is why, according to Rudolf Steiner, those who know how to work with these things with care and reverence will be able to find much about the soul and destiny of the deceased in a death horoscope.* In this connection, however, the degree to which we knew the deceased as a person is important.

During a first phase of the way from death to a new birth (when there is still a connection with the etheric body), we leave the physical world in accordance with the starry constellations that were important in our life, especially those at the moment of death. During these days we are filled with pictures of our life that arise in us as our life tableau, which reflect our experiences during waking life. Once those pictures have faded, in the second phase we begin to adapt to our spiritual form and thus seek our way into the world of spirit through what, to us at our death, is the East. Why the East specifically—the direction of

* Rudolf Steiner, *The Karma of Untruthfulness*, vol. 2, p. 157.

the rising Sun? The soul follows the etheric body that seeks the Sun in its integration into the etheric world. It has an old and deep connection with the Sun; it is at home there. Our present Sun is a living reminder of an older stage of life of our universe, the pre-earthly, Ancient Sun; you could also say "occult Sun," where our etheric body was created. When we are on the way and want to come to terms with our recent past, we are looking for the source of life forces in our past. (See also appendix 3 on the developmental stages of the universe and Earth.)

Through the East, we definitively leave the physical world and in the third phase enter the world of spirit. We then step into the spiritual domain of the globe. Whereas we have a centrifugal orientation directed toward the cosmos, away from the Earth during life, after death we have an opportunity in the fourth phase to work toward the Earth. From the other side of the portals of the East, those who have died exert their influence on the Earth in a centripetal way; the Earth is the center of their cosmos.

These are the four phases of beginning the way from death to a new birth, the way that leads us into the world of spirit. What is briefly sketched here is a very long and often painful process for the dead. The first phase was described in my book *What Happens after We Die;* here we want to begin by exploring the subsequent phases. Before we can do this, however, we have to consider a few more aspects.

Sleep and Death

Sleep is sometimes called death's younger brother. Indeed, at first glance sleep and death have much in common; standing next to a deceased body we might even think it is still breathing lightly. Both a sleeping person and a deceased person are unreachable for us; they are "elsewhere" and have no obvious connection with us. Steiner once said that the only difference between sleep and death is in consciousness.* During sleep we are not conscious of ourselves or of the outer world, whereas after death we are.

As is so often the case, more could be said about this, despite the categorical sound of this statement. Looked at more closely, it turns out that the similarity between sleep and death in other respects is not all that deep. For instance, in both sleep and death, the unity of the astral body and "I" with the physical and etheric bodies is broken. During sleep, the astral body separates and lives within the earthly cosmos, returning to the body on waking, when the physical and etheric bodies absorb it again. However, in death the astral body loosens itself from the physical body and does not separate from the etheric body until after a few days. Because of its connection with the astral body, the "I" during waking life is oriented toward the sensory world, from which it frees itself only after death. It can then direct itself to the world of spirit.

Therefore, in sleep as well as in death the connection of the spiritual human being in his astral body and "I" with the physical person is broken—temporarily in sleep and definitively in death. Whereas in sleep the astral body and "I" nevertheless maintain a connection with the physical person in the physical world, at death they begin to connect themselves with world of spirit. But Steiner showed that these differences in orientation go much deeper than we would suspect.

Rudolf Steiner's insights into the world of spirit give us decisive explanations about the difference between sleep and

* Rudolf Steiner, *Between Death and Rebirth*, p. 76.

death in a surprising way. We have already seen that the spiritual world we enter in sleep is different from the one we enter after death. What is the story about these two world of spirit? To understand this, let's look again at the incarnated human being on Earth.

During life on Earth, we live in space and time and add to this a certain degree of consciousness. We live in three dimensions of space, time, and consciousness and recognize this threefoldness in the three directions of space—length, width, and height—as well as the three aspects of time (past, present, and future). In addition to our waking, dreaming, and sleeping states of consciousness, we suspect a "spiritual" consciousness, higher consciousness that gives us access to the world of spirit.

Two Spiritual Worlds

In contrast to what the dogma of materialism wants us to believe, the world of our waking consciousness—that of the senses—only seems material. It is a world of phenomena, comparable to a rainbow, which sometimes appears to the eye almost tangible and concrete, but is still a phenomenon. We all know that the rainbow is an optical phenomenon within a tangible reality. Similarly, this tangible, sensory world is one of tangible phenomena, in which and behind which spiritual beings live and work. When we turn to the outside in our waking consciousness, we encounter a sensory world of phenomena, and only behind it can we suspect a reality; that reality consists of spiritual beings.

Now, we can also go inside, into our own inner world. What kind of world do we find there? Usually we can't go very far because we get hung up in our memories, non-material phenomena. Pious souls and mystics expected to find the Spirit there or behind it—God, the divine spark. Well, we can find all kinds of things in there, but unfortunately no spirit. Within ourselves, we find no spiritual but only material processes, and the spark we find when we go into ourselves is the product of organic processes. The spark requires material processes to exist, much like the flame of a candle. When we go inside, we are faced with a spiritual world of phenomena, and the material realities in and behind it. We find organic processes there, and in their effects the specifically material aspects of our earthly existence.

A spiritual world that hides behind sensory phenomena outside ourselves and a material world behind spiritual phenomena within ourselves—Rudolf Steiner helps us again, seemingly turning things upside down to overcome our cherished images and prejudices.

When we fall asleep we leave in our astral body and "I"; the physical and etheric bodies remain behind in the bed. Where then do we go? Certainly not inside and into our inner world. While sleeping we enter the spiritual world hidden behind the sensory world. This is the world that generates the world of the senses. Waking up, we return to the world of the senses.

When we die we leave the world that appears in such a variety of ways in three dimensions, and enter the world of spirit that we left at birth. We cannot look for it behind the sensory world because, although it is related to this, it is yet essentially different. When dying we leave space and enter into pure time, the world that generates us as human beings, the world where we find our origin in the spirit, the world that pushes us out again into a subsequent incarnation. On Earth we live in a "spiritual outside world" that is sensory, and in a "material inside world" within ourselves. When dying we enter our "spiritual home world," the world of the nine heavenly hierarchies.

To characterize these two spiritual worlds Rudolf Steiner used the concepts *centrifugal* and *centripetal.** Centripetal is the world behind that of the senses; here, spiritual beings who seek the center are working. It is a cold, rigidifying, calcifying world. The other spiritual world is centrifugal because forces are working there that repel and scatter. Without the centripetal forces this world would endlessly expand and scatter. The heavenly hierarchies that are at home in this centrifugal world ("the gods," Rudolf Steiner sometimes called them) stand only through the human being in perceptible contact with the centripetal world, which is foreign to them. Thanks to the human being something of soul warmth comes into that icy world. It is only because the human being is connected with the centripetal world that the gods can keep their centrifugal world together.

In this way the human being is involved with two extremes, with two worlds of diverging forces, with diverging spiritual beings therefore. Only within the human being, who acts as intermediary in this, do these forces, these so different spiritual beings meet. In this function as intermediary the human being finds his cosmic task. The human being himself belongs to the world of the creative gods, of the nine hierarchies; in their world, which we enter after death, we find our origin and our purpose. In the centripetal world we find the web of our own destiny that the angels have woven for us, and day after day we spin there the many threads for the new web we take with us into death.

---

* Rudolf Steiner, *Spiritual Science as a Foundation for Social Forms*, p. 172.

From Outer to Inner Experiences

How do we take this web of destiny with us into death? The introduction mentioned that our true "I" and the astral body do not really incarnate but remain behind in our prebirth existence. What we call our "I" and astral body reflect these in the physical body. As we have seen, when we sleep these reflections dwell in the spiritual world that underlies the physical world. When asleep we go through the experiences of our waking life once again, now in reverse sequence and colored by a moral judgment. In this way we end up at the beginning of the past day's experiences by the time we wake up. In sleep we go to our true "I" and astral body, which have remained in the other spiritual world, and we let them share in our backward review of all that happened that day. Thus we go back through time to the beginning of our life, yes, even further back to what preceded it.

By the way, reflecting on the role of sleep in our moral inner life, we come across one of the many paradoxical truths we are so often confronted with in Rudolf Steiner's work. Do we fall asleep because we have become tired? Or do we become tired because we want to fall asleep and communicate with our true "I" and astral body? The latter, said Rudolf Steiner; people fall asleep whether or not they are tired.* Again and again the will takes charge so as to bring order into destiny.

When, after dying, the pictures of the life tableau have faded away, we stand at the point where our life began. Now, however, we are filled with all that happened during our entire life. Now the moment has come when we can really go back through our whole life, with the aid of everything we have experienced in the nightly backward reviews during sleep. In doing so we move, in

* Rudolf Steiner, *Cosmosophy*, vol. 2, Nov. 12, 1921.

the sense of what was described before, to the East, away from the Earth in the direction shown by the etheric body.

We have seen how we human beings are connected throughout our lives with those so different spiritual worlds, and it seems that this leads us to the reason why the astral body and "I" do not actually incarnate. For they have nothing in common with the centripetal world that chills and rigidifies, to which we have to descend for the sake of our further journey to become human. They do not leave the centrifugal world with its angels, and during life we have to make do with their reflections. Nevertheless we succeed in bringing to the true "I" and astral body during sleep the harvest of our waking human consciousness. Our earthly experiences become inner experiences; from a spiritual outside world they are transferred to the world that is our spiritual home. In this way what was conveyed in sleep during life can gradually be processed and made an integral part of our "I" after death.

The Members of the Human Being

Let us look again at the human being as we have come to know him in his fourfold nature of 1) physical body, 2) etheric body, 3) astral body, and 4) "I." What was not discussed were three still hidden, but in principle already present members to be formed as the "I," working out of the spirit, transforms the three bodies: 5) *spirit self*, the transformed astral body, 6) *life spirit*, the transformed etheric body, and 7) *spirit body*, the transformed physical body. We find this sevenfold nature described at the end of Rudolf Steiner's book *Theosophy*, his first book about the suprasensory aspects of the human being.*

* Rudolf Steiner, *Theosophy*, "The Essential Nature of the Human Being," pp. 53ff. *Geistesmensch*, or "spirit human being," is the physical body transformed by the "I"—the "spirit body."

With the term *astral body,* Steiner alludes to what transcends sensory perception. It is the body in which a part of our soul has taken "form." The astral body is a whole consisting of *soul body* and *sentient soul*, the part of the soul into which we actively receive and process impressions. Besides the soul that lives in impressions we have the *intellectual soul* that enables us to think. The heart of human consciousness is called *consciousness soul.* Intellectual soul and consciousness soul are two sheaths of the "I" that belong together; the "I" is the core of both. Just as the soul body and the sentient soul together form a unity, so do the consciousness soul and spirit self.

We now have a picture before us of the nine members of the entire human being: 1) physical body, 2) etheric body, 3) astral or soul body, 4) sentient soul, 5) intellectual soul, 6) consciousness, or spiritual, soul, 7) spirit self, 8) life spirit, and 9) spirit body. We can also picture earthly man with seven members, by combining into a unity the astral body and sentient soul as well as the consciousness soul and spirit self.

In the fourfold picture of the human being, the earthly part is comprised of the physical and etheric bodies, whereas the spiritual human is represented by the astral body and the "I," which form the soul. In the soul, the "I" represents the spirit, while body and soul are connected in the astral body. In the sevenfold picture we see the transition from body to soul in the perceptive soul body, and the transition from soul to spirit in the spirit-filled consciousness soul (which is also the core of the "I"). Finally, in the ninefold picture of the complete human being the body is represented by the physical, etheric, and astral bodies, the soul by the sentient, intellectual, and consciousness souls, and the spirit by the spirit self, life spirit, and spirit body.

Rudolf Steiner once summarized it all as follows.* The physical, etheric, and astral bodies represent our cosmic past in us. Our future lies in what the "I" can make of this as it transforms these members into spirit self, life spirit, and spirit body. In the "I" we experience our present. The "I" itself is a threefold entity because the soul has three aspects. It consists of three fundamental forces that we know as sentient soul, intellectual soul, and consciousness soul. These are part of the individuality that gradually comes to full consciousness. We can also call them intelligence, individuality and morality. In the sentient soul, we feel the soul in an inner way; the astral body can be considered as the outside, the exterior of the sentient soul. The "I," as it comes to consciousness, wrests itself free from the intellectual soul. Within the growing forces of the "I," the consciousness soul is experienced as inner and the spirit self as outer.

The way from death to a new birth begins when the dead body is left behind in the physical world and the retrospect of life rises as the life panorama. Similarly, the deceased leaves a kind of second corpse behind when the etheric body is given over to the elemental world; then the second phase of the journey begins, the time of purification and processing. At the end of this period, the untransformed part of the astral body will be left behind as a third corpse. At this point, all corporeality will have been thrown off, and the deceased can enter a new phase, the third on the way; thus, all that reminds us of a body will have disappeared. I now want to follow Rudolf Steiner's terminology and, in lieu of the words *deceased* and *dead,* use the word *soul,* emphasizing in this way that it is important to recognize the dead already in the soul existence at the

* Rudolf Steiner, *Die Mission der neuen Geistesoffenbarung*, June 14, 1911.

beginning of the second phase. Later we will have to speak of "the human being." But in the world of spirit, the human is always a being-in-becoming. During life it may sometimes look as if we are inwardly "silted up." With death we enter a domain where everything is becoming and developing. Immersed in this domain permeated by spiritual solar forces, we begin a journey of becoming that leads to a new birth.

Without the Sun, to which the soul directs itself inwardly at the beginning of this journey from death to a new birth, we could not have lived on Earth. In one of his meditative verses, written in September 1924, Rudolf Steiner expressed our relationship to the Sun in a tremendous image. Let us take this picture with us now that we want to follow the deceased on their way to the worlds of soul and spirit.

> Look, you my eye,
> the Sun's pure rays
> from earth's formations.
>
> Look, you my heart,
> the Sun's spirit forces
> from water's ripples.
>
> Look, you my soul,
> the Sun's cosmic will
> from air's glimmering shine.
>
> Look, you my spirit,
> the Sun's gods
> from the fire of love.*

* Rudolf Steiner, *Verses and Meditations*, p. 141 (trans. revised).

2

The Soul World

It must have been a wonderful time when the "one true Church" had a solid grip on all souls. How simple life was in those days. You knew your situation, even when it came to death. You knew about heaven, where every decent person eventually ended up. If you had anything bad on your record (and who didn't?), you would have to spend time in purgatory. In that place of purification, the faithful had to suffer for a while to atone for their sins. If you had gone too far, you ended up in hell, the place of the damned, a place of terror, where sinners would be punished for their crimes in a blazing fire. Then there was limbo, where the just would await the coming of Christ. You were sent there if, through no fault of your own, you missed the blessings of the Church—for example, by dying before you were baptized.

These medieval pictures gave people a lot of clarity after the obscure existence in an underworld into which people in ancient times saw their deceased disappear after their death. The Greeks saw their dead spend their existence without any life forces in Hades, the Jews in Sheol. Then Christ appeared; he broke the underworld open and gave the dead a real chance again. The new hope with which people viewed death, however, was quickly put into fixed channels by the Roman Church. Even for those in limbo, membership in the Church was of decisive importance. One became a member by being baptized. True, one's own behavior and one's own inner strength could play a modest role in the choice between hell and purgatory as the vestibule to heaven.

In this way, one's life after death was simply a straightforward continuation of one's life on Earth. Those who belonged to the Church had a chance to have a decent existence after death, especially if one made sure of getting preferential treatment by buying indulgences. Thus the original dynamic of the question "Why do you seek the living among the dead?" effectively ran aground within the bureaucracy of the Church. The soul actually went into a kind of retirement after death, for no real activity was needed on the part of the people themselves to collaborate on what they brought with them into death.

Sukie Miller's book, *After Death,* contains an inventory of pictures and ideas about life after death from the most different cultures. She traveled all over the world and learned much from the Delaware Indians in the United States, the inhabitants of Bali and Sulawesi in Indonesia, various peoples in Africa, and Aborigines in Australia. She also became familiar with the traditions of various great religions, from Hinduism to Islam. Inevitably, we find ripe and unripe ideas mixed together in her reports, from ancient wisdom to untested imaginations. When she reviews her material, she distinguishes four stages in life after death. To some extent we can recognize them from what we find in Rudolf Steiner's work.

During the first stage, she discovered, those who have died spend time in a kind of heavenly waiting room. It is a place of transition where one comes to rest, a place of purification and transformation. The next stage is the one of penance and judgment, where one's further destiny is formed, a place of evaluation and confrontation with truth. In the third stage, the future opens according to the possibilities of one's destiny; one enters heaven or hell and sojourns with their inhabitants. The fourth stage is that of return; here, reincarnation becomes a fact, although the religions of the Book officially still reject this.

These four stages seem to reflect the traditional canvas of Western images, supplemented by the idea of reincarnation. The author realizes at the end that the motivation that helps us along in life, whether here on Earth or after death, is hope. This is not something we encounter often in traditional Christian views, but it did exist during the first few centuries of Christianity.

Faith, Love, Hope

Faith, love, and hope, said the apostle Paul, are the three strong powers in the soul that help us on a path that leads upward. They are durable and remain when all else has fallen away and culminate in love (1 Cor. 13). Steiner, too, knew these three powers of the soul, which are so fundamental that the soul can never be deprived of them. They point the way for those who can no longer live with the black-and-white scheme that reserves eternal bliss for those who do good and eternal damnation for those who do evil. They appear in Rudolf Steiner's work in a surprising light.

Faith can be a lot more than simply believing in something that I cannot know is a fact. We can believe in someone; we can believe in something that far exceeds our own existence. With faith we reach for and begin to move toward something higher. Faith is the power of courage in the soul, as Emil Bock once said.* When we cannot believe, our soul has to shrivel up. Faith lives in our astral body, the first sheath of the "I," and it continually bestows life force on the soul. This is why Rudolf Steiner called the astral body our "faith body" or "faith soul."

* Emil Bock, *The Rhythm of the Christian Year.*

Love is the highest power in the soul; it is like light in which we humans can inwardly breathe, light that warms our world, fiery and radiant. No one can do without love; no one can truly live without loving. Those who cannot love dry up and wither in their soul. Love has its home in the etheric body, our "love body," the sunny sheath that bears both the "I" and the astral body.

Those who cannot hope are very badly off; their world is closed and life is hopeless. Hope feeds life, no matter how much it may sound like a cliché. Always hoping, we find what makes life durable, the constants of existence: "Seedtime and harvest, cold and heat, summer and winter, day and night shall not cease while the Earth remains" (Gen. 8:22). Our other members are enveloped and carried by the physical body, our "body of hope." Thanks to hope we strive to endure for a certain measure of permanence. Those who cannot hope will see themselves perish like an annual plant at the beginning of winter.

During life we are able to live in these three sheaths, the three "bodies" of soul power. When we leave the physical body behind, we also leave the physical expression of our "body of hope." Is it an exaggeration to suspect that in the realm of spiritual formative forces, into which we submerge with lightning speed, we enter a world of hope that gives the soul strength on its way to the world of spirit? When our etheric body then unites with the etheric world, the web of our destiny is taken up into a "world of love." Still carried by the power of faith in our astral body and through the forces of courage in the "faith body," we begin the honest and open confrontation with the life that has just stood before us in the life panorama. During life, faith, hope, and love worked as powers in the soul. After death they unlock worlds, spiritual domains; they help the soul find its way in its very own world, which begins to dawn in kamaloka.

The Soul in Kamaloka

Kamaloka is one of the few words from Indian theosophy that remained in use in Anthroposophy. In his book *Theosophy,* Rudolf Steiner wrote in chapter 3, "The Three Worlds," that this part of the soul world can be called "the place of desires." In the Christian tradition we know this place of desires as purgatory. The advantage of a word like *kamaloka* is that it does not generally evoke any associations in us Westerners and receives its meaning for us from what Steiner said and wrote about it.

The journey of the soul through kamaloka is one of detaching and processing. Steiner described this from various viewpoints. Let's begin with the oldest description, the one in his book *Theosophy,* written in 1904.* We first find a description of the "soul world" in chapter 3, "The Three Worlds," and then one of the soul's experiences in the "soul in the soul world after death." When Steiner looks back at these descriptions later on, he emphasizes the effort he took to convey a feeling of what the soul goes through.

The soul sojourns in kamaloka so long as it has not yet overcome and transformed its ties to the life just ended. During that time, our inner world arises around us with all our desires and wishes, all our feelings and moods. Consequently, we are imprisoned within ourselves, as it were, and only gradually (indeed very gradually) we find that we cannot break out of our prison unless we succeed in transforming our wishes, desires, and moods. A radical "turning inside out" of our inner world awaits us.

---

* Rudolf Steiner, *Theosophy*, pp. 93ff.

Every time it is again a shock to realize how differently we have to learn to think if we want to understand the experiences of the soul in kamaloka. Let's not forget; kamaloka is part of the soul world, the part in which we are in quarantine, so to speak. To describe what happens in the soul world to us, when our inner world has become our outside, we have to grope for pictures from the physical world. To describe the realities of that world, Rudolf Steiner used a word that can best be rendered as "soul form." Soul forms consist, one could say, of soul substance, something more malleable, mobile, and finer than what the word *substance* evokes in the physical world.

In the physical world, the mutual relationships of substances depend on their density, whether solid, liquid, or gaseous. In the soul world, the interaction among soul forms depends on their affinity; they interpenetrate if they are related to one another and repel each other if they are strangers. Whereas in our physical world perspective depends on whether things seem to be close to each other or far away, in the soul world the "distance" between souls depends on their degree of affinity.

What assumes a solid, liquid, or gaseous form in the physical world appears as sympathy or antipathy in the soul world. With sympathy, soul forms attract each other; they interpenetrate and melt into each other. Antipathy causes them to exclude one another and remain solitary. In the first three regions of kamaloka, affection and aversion are present and work in ever-changing proportions in the soul forms we encounter there.

Gradually, in kamaloka, antipathy is overcome in the soul until the soul becomes all sympathy. At that point, the soul has overcome its inclination toward a physical, sensory existence and can become one with the soul world. Then the spirit is also freed from its ties to the soul.

The First Three Soul Regions

First we should distinguish among three kinds of soul forms, depending on the way sympathy and antipathy are active. The first, which we encounter in kamaloka, creates the impression of being dominated completely by antipathy; any existing sympathy disappears almost entirely into nothingness. Such a soul form is egoistic; it repels virtually everything and attracts little. It comes across as greedy and grasping; the sympathy that is present in it can never be satisfied, because the ever-predominating antipathy repels everything. It gives the impression of being unchangeable and reminds us of solid material bodies of the physical world. The part of the soul world where such forms are at home is the *region of burning desire*. The soul stays here until all that lives in it as desires and passions, "the soul's crudest, self-serving desires," have been burned off.*

Sensory desires can always be satisfied during life. When satisfaction becomes impossible and there is nothing left that can be satisfied by sensory means, pains of burning desire torment the soul for as long as it takes them to consume themselves. People without much lust and desire pass through this region rather easily, since they have no affinity with it. To the degree that their affinity is greater, souls have to spend more time in this region of purification, longing for the extirpation of one of their imperfections. Purification is not just suffering; it also brings relief. It is indeed a relief to shake off the desire for sensory stimulation and to stop longing for the senses.

There is a balance between sympathy and antipathy in the second of these first three soul forms. These forms create a

* Ibid., pp. 115–117.

"neutral" impression; they don't seem to have clear boundaries or real "skin." They can be compared to liquid substances on Earth. It is not a matter of desire but a kind of neutral, selfless receptivity. This is the *region of flowing sensitivity*, where those who led a superficial life, fluttering from futility to futility, have to remain for a while. It is painful to do without the fleeting and scanty satisfactions we used to have. When we overcome this, we also free ourselves from the illusions that have captivated us during life. In this region of purification the soul is also freed from its craving for thoughts bound to the physical instrument of the brain. It is a relief that one no longer has to think in the way one had to do on Earth.

In the third soul form that is encountered, sympathy has become stronger than antipathy. The tendency to assert oneself becomes overshadowed by the inclination to open oneself. Consequently, these soul forms can manifest as the center of a sphere that attracts and encompasses all of the surroundings. They have the tendency to expand in all directions, just as earthly gaseous substances do. They form the *region of wishes*. Because of the still present but weak antipathy these soul forms not only want to attract, but they also want to incorporate things into themselves; so for this reason, their sympathy still has an egoistic undertone.

All that still lives in the soul as wishes brings it under the influence of this region. But since these wishes cannot be satisfied, they gradually have to die off. In this region of purification the soul leaves behind every wish that keeps it fettered to life on Earth. It is a relief to be content without having to nurture such wishes any longer.

The Soul in the Soul World

After these three soul forms, the soul becomes acquainted with higher levels of the soul world and its own soul forms. In the fourth soul form, antipathy has completely disappeared, with only the other fundamental force remaining. The soul forms in this region are completely united with feelings; sympathy works strongly as lust, weakly as disgust, and thus determines the feeling of wellbeing in the *region of pleasure and displeasure.* Particular trials await us here because we identify with our body owing to such feelings during life. The self-awareness this gives us is like being hollowed out after death; we lose ourselves, one could say. This is why we have to lose the illusion of our bodily existence specifically and be cured of all longing for the body. In this way the soul is cured of itself. Then the soul world opens to it, for at this point the soul has been freed of all longing for the body that served it on Earth.

In a letter written in 1905, Rudolf Steiner described what the soul goes through on its way through the first regions of the soul world.* When he did this he also gave a meditative verse to accompany the deceased:

May my love be the sheaths
that now surround you—
cooling your warmth,
warming your cold—
intertwined through sacrifice,
live, carried upward by love,
gifted with light! . . .**

---

* Letter to Paula Stryczek of Dec. 31, 1905, *From the History and Content of the First Esoteric School 1904–1914*, pp. 102–104 (also quoted in my book *What Happens after We Die*, p. 108).

** Rudolf Steiner, *Our Dead*, p. 331.

In his letter, Rudolf Steiner pointed out that we need the right feeling for the words "warmth" and "cold." This is not physical warmth and cold, but a feeling sense of warmth and cold, something difficult to imagine for those who acknowledge feelings only as expressions of the soul and not as conditions. In kamaloka, forces of the soul are still present and active without being anchored in the body, with no possibility of realizing them through physical instruments. The fact that the soul has to exist without physical instruments evokes something like a feeling of burning thirst, coupled with a strong experience of warmth. On the other hand, the will was especially accustomed to expressing itself immediately, but now it has to do without that. This causes a feeling like cold in the soul.

We have to realize, however, that the condition in which the deceased find themselves in kamaloka is only partly the consequence of an individual's way of life. The detachment that needs to be achieved does not depend completely on the way we have lived. The fact that we have lived—that we needed a body to live—has a long-lasting effect. All those who have been embodied on Earth need kamaloka to free themselves from the grip of all that is earthly.

When the soul leaves the region of pleasure and displeasure it has left the painful part of kamaloka behind. It has freed itself of the self-woven web in which it had been imprisoned. It enters a soul world that does not consist of separate soul forms. Since there is no longer any antipathy, the soul no longer needs to be self-oriented to strengthen and enrich itself at the expense of something or someone else. Souls that have overcome self-centered feelings are open to the radiance, the revelation of what is other. They have found one communal soul world, the substance of which is like the light in which we can feel ourselves bathed—radiant, active, life giving.

The Actual Soul World

The first part of the higher soul world, the fifth soul region, is the *region of soul light.* The power of sympathy begins to shine out from the soul being in streams as of light. The soul grows to the extent it is able inwardly to connect with this soul space, and can free its ideals from every sensory component. Raving about nature and pursuing sensory wellbeing have to be overcome. The same is true for religious feelings that strive to go to heaven, or paradise. Whoever seeks paradise finds it here—and also realizes that in this way it is of no value. The task in this region is to cleanse moral, supra-personal ideals from every sensory impression.

The "unpleasant" aspect of kamaloka is now gone, but that does not mean that all suffering is behind us. In this region the moral constitution of the soul determines whether the soul can connect, whether it can be a social being or has to lead the existence of a kind of hermit. An asocial, immoral life keeps the soul imprisoned in itself and causes its exclusion from community with the inhabitants of this region.

Sometimes there is more; in such higher regions, unscrupulous people may come to depend on truly evil spirits. There are spiritual beings who direct the appearance of epidemics on Earth, such as notorious past incidents of cholera or plague. They also cause people to die too early because of illness or accidents. People who went through life without much sense of responsibility or conscience have a difficult time in this soul region. They are condemned to serve such frightful evil spirits of illness and death for a while and have to help them achieve their goals.

Indolence and laziness in life condemns people in this soul region to become servants of a different kind of evil power. These are the spirits who set up hurdles and pitfalls and who want to obstruct development on Earth. (In appendix 6 we get to know them as ahrimanic powers.) Laziness in thinking or action leads to subservience to such obstructive spirits for a time.

In the *region of active soul power*, the soul must be cleansed of its craving for satisfaction through the performance of deeds. In this sixth soul region, the initially sluggish and dull activity of the soul begins to become mobile and to shine. The sensory component in the striving of an artist or scientist, for instance, must be overcome here and left behind. Whether human beings can be at home in this region and can find community with like-minded souls depends on the religious ground of the soul. Those who have been unable to believe in the eternal and imperishable and who were unable to turn in faith toward the Godhead remain imprisoned in themselves and lack any form of community. Thanks to its religious disposition, the soul comes into contact with the angels of the higher hierarchies here and, consequently, achieves the inner freedom of movement it needs.

The *region of soul life* is the seventh and highest region of the soul world. Here the soul frees itself of its last ties to the sensory, physical world. The subtlest materialism, which looks for uses of the spirit in the physical world, is exorcised. Those who know that life and work have to be oriented toward the eternal and imperishable will be at home in this region. The important matter here is whether the soul has been able to understand not just like-minded people but all human beings. Every prejudice keeps the soul imprisoned in itself; lack of understanding and having to be separated from others are sources of pain. In this region the soul will finally be able to become completely itself.

Kamaloka

To cleanse itself of the consequences of its life on Earth, the soul has sojourned for a shorter or longer time in the regions with which it felt a relationship; it remained there for as long as it took to overcome those consequences. It quietly passed by the regions with which it had no relationship. In the lower regions of the soul world, shortly after death, the primary purpose was to purify the feelings and impulses of will that limited it to the earthly world of experience. As the soul overcame its earthly orientation, it divested itself of any need for earthly instruments. In the higher regions of the soul world, the soul could grow only insofar as it could connect with its own world and break out of its self-created prison.

Rudolf Steiner made numerous comments about the time the soul spends in kamaloka. For this period of detachment and processing we need roughly a third of the time our life on Earth lasted—approximately the time we spend sleeping during life. This is related to the fact that we are actually rather fond of our body, but as the day progresses we begin to tire of it. Steiner reminded us of this when he spoke to the workers at the Goetheanum in 1923.* Babies are never tired of their bodies; they love to bask in the delicious feeling that their digestion evokes in them. This is the reason they sleep so much and wake as soon as they are hungry again. As adults, we want to sleep out of antipathy toward the body we have used all day. We sleep as long as it takes to overcome

* Rudolf Steiner, *From Limestone to Lucifer...*, p. 78.

this antipathy in the soul and feel sympathy for it again so that we can wake up.

After we have died we have to begin to overcome our sympathy for the body. Just as during life we spend roughly a third of every twenty-four-hour day to regenerate sympathy for the body, likewise we need a third of our lifespan for the opposite, in which the degree to which we have loved our body also plays a role. In the successive levels of the soul world we discover how this was with us and learn the detachment we need.

In kamaloka we also process what we experienced during life as the first step toward correcting our destiny. Each night during sleep we look back at our daytime experiences, revisiting all we did and all that happened to us during the day, making it our own and looking at it from a moral point of view. When we wake up, we sometimes have an aftertaste of this. Then we can begin the day in a better way. (I return to this in the conclusion).

In kamaloka we go through our life in the same retrograde direction as we do during the nights, which requires around the same amount of time—a third of our lifespan. In this process we especially experience the effects of our actions for other people in the world. How we go through our experiences and the life we lived depends in part on the way we are able to make our way through the levels of the soul world. However, a remnant of antipathy will remain in the soul, which we take with us into our next life. This is what we have to try to overcome in our spiritual relationships with others—in our common language, in mental images and thoughts we share with others, and in the arts and religion. This form of antipathy rears its head in all forms of sectarianism.

In his book *Theosophy,* Rudolf Steiner gave a general sketch of the soul world and the soul's inner experiences there. In a lecture cycle in 1912/13, he described this "from the outside."* After showing the way of the soul toward the spirit as a journey through time, he described it in his lectures as a journey into the cosmos. Let's look at this spatial aspect.

The Planetary Spheres

The heavens and the stars provide the background for the movements of the Moon and planets. We all know them, at least by their names. Closest to the Earth is the Moon, the satellite of the Earth, and then Venus and Mercury, the so-called inner planets because their distance from the Sun is less than that of the Earth. The outer planets are farther from the Sun than the Earth is; the orbits of Mars, Jupiter, and Saturn circle both the Earth and the Sun, never passing between the Sun and Earth. Uranus, Neptune, and Pluto will not be considered here, since they are not visible to the naked eye; thus they are not part of "our" cosmos.

We must understand that Copernicus created a calculable universe when he realized that the Sun is the center of our system of Sun and planets; we will let that be what it is, for if we want to follow what Rudolf Steiner described, we have to "turn around" again and find our standpoint on the Earth. In doing so, we do not consider the Earth one of the planets revolving around the Sun, but we do view the Moon as one. We base ourselves on what we can observe—the phenomena of "outer appearance." We discover then that the Greeks expressed the qualities of the various planets very well through their names. Venus makes a different impression on us from that of Mercury; every planet has a specific quality. Nonetheless, in this

* Rudolf Steiner, *Between Death and Rebirth,* Dec. 10, 1912.

incalculable universe, the planet itself is only an indication or landmark that indicates for us the boundary between two areas. We can try to follow the complete visible course of a planet to imagine its orbit. This gives us an idea of the limits of its sphere, which fills the entire space within the limit of its orbit, allowing us to imagine it as a kind of three-dimensional, "spatial body."

The sphere of the Moon becomes visible through its orbit around the Earth. In the case of the next two planets, we have to realize that their names were switched through the course of centuries. The planet we call Venus was called Mercury in ancient spiritual traditions, and today's Mercury, viewed spiritually, is Venus. Thus, we identify spiritual Venus with astronomical Mercury, and spiritual Mercury with astronomical Venus. Viewed spiritually, Mercury is closer to the Earth than Venus is.

The sphere of the Moon is enclosed within the sphere of Mercury, the sphere that follows that of the Moon; both of these, in turn, are enclosed within the sphere of Venus. The Sun sphere permeates the spheres of all three of these planets. The spheres of Mars, Jupiter, and Saturn, as their orbits show, are progressively larger, and only that of Saturn is not permeated by other, larger spheres.

After death, the soul that makes its way through the various regions of the soul world also moves through these planetary spheres. It spends the painful part of kamaloka in the Moon sphere, in the three regions of burning desire, streaming receptivity, and wishes. As its purification progresses in the region of pleasure and displeasure, it gradually expands into the sphere of Mercury. In the region of soul light in the Mercury sphere, the actual soul world opens itself to it. The soul then goes through the region of active soul force in the Venus sphere, and the region of soul life opens itself to it in the Sun sphere.

Upon entering these regions, the soul begins the third phase of the course on which the human being leaves Earth and adapts to the cosmos. It "goes toward the Sun" to enter the spiritual domain of the globe that is preeminently the cosmic body.

In the Mars, Jupiter, and Saturn spheres the soul will enter the first regions of the realm of spirit, enriched by what it can take with it from the Sun sphere. These are the spheres we first reach and come to know in the next chapter.

3

The World of Spirit

We have stood by the deathbed, next to the body left behind by the deceased, and have followed the soul as its passes through the various regions of kamaloka. In a painful process of detachment, the experiences gained in the world, thanks to the body, are sorted out, purified, and worked through there. We saw how the soul, as it succeeds in leaving behind all that is a burden to it, gradually comes to feel at home in its own world, the soul world. In the seventh and highest level of the soul world, the region of soul life, the soul will have finally grown fully into its own way of existence. Then, in the Sun sphere, the final remnants of what still ties the spirit to the soul are overcome. The spirit can then enter its own world, the realm of spirit, which we can view as the first area of our future homeland that we reach on our way from death to a new birth. Here we truly have to live into this world to prepare for another embodiment, our subsequent homeland.

The world of spirit is a realm of spirits (Rudolf Steiner often called it "spirit land") and, like the soul world, it has seven regions, or layers. To prepare properly for the next incarnation, what we have gained on Earth must be transformed into living capacities of spirit. That is not possible unless the spirit is in constant development here; it goes through a continuous education and eventually works completely through its experiences gained in prior lives. Immersing itself in the several levels of spirit land, the spirit temporarily adopts their characteristics, merging into them as if in a mutual osmosis.

The realm of spirits is a world in which substance is formed by living thoughts that are spiritual beings. These are the spiritual archetypes of everything that has received form in the physical and soul worlds. However, let us not confuse these archetypes with their reflections—which are the abstract thoughts with which we are familiar. We can be thoroughly mixed up when we see them, because the archetypes do not look at all like what they have generated and, moreover, they are also in constant movement. The whole realm of spirit is creative movement; archetypes are interconnected in ever-changing configurations. They "bud" without interruption, and once they have "sprouted " another being immediately announces itself. A spiritual archetype is able to generate, usually together with others, a never-ending multiplicity of individual forms that can be "seen" and "heard." Spiritual archetypes are also "archetypal tones," oceans of sounds in which the observer is embedded, but they can also be observed in various ways in a kind of "spiritual tasting."

Earlier we saw that everything takes place in the soul world at a deeply inner level, and that it depends on the mutual affinity among soul forms. The word *level* certainly does not mean "layer" in this context—regions of the soul world are not layered but interpenetrate and flow into one another. This is also true for the realm of spirit, in which we must not imagine things next to or outside one another. Regions, or levels, inter-permeate as the planetary spheres have been described; the upper level permeates all the lower ones, and the lowest is permeated by all the higher levels. This is why human beings experience only a "subsequent level" when they have acquired capacities to become aware of its characteristics. We do not "ascend" when we reach a higher level; we perceive there what has surrounded us all along. So that we do not to forget this, let's not say *at* this level, but *in* this level as we follow the soul and spirit on their way through the various levels. Further along, however, I use the concepts "ascent" and "descent" to characterize succinctly the way we pass through the planetary spheres. The image of our ascent on our way to the midpoint of the time between death and rebirth and then our descent includes the idea that this midpoint is not in the same level for all human souls.

In the realm of spirit, we are in the kitchen, so to speak, where everything is prepared that we came to know in the physical world. The picture Plato used can help us imagine how this works. To describe our relationship with reality, he used the image of a cave in which people are chained so they cannot move and can look only straight ahead at the rear wall of the cave. Behind them, a great fire is burning at the cave's entrance, while figures between the fire and them move and cast shadows on the rear wall of the cave. Those shadows are the only reality that these people can see. They don't realize that a fire is burning behind them and that there are figures moving and casting shadows on the wall. Given their situation, they are forced to believe that the shadows before them are the only reality.*

According to the cave analogy, during life on Earth we are aware of only the shadows, the reflections of the realities that move "behind" us—the spiritual archetypes. Rudolf Steiner picked up on this image, it seems, when he wrote that during life we know only the shadows of those spiritual archetypes; they come to consciousness in us through our thinking.**

If we can "turn around" during our life we would find ourselves in the midst of those realities themselves. This happens

* See, for example, Porphyry, *On the Cave of the Nymphs.*

** Rudolf Steiner, *Between Death and Rebirth,* Dec. 10, 1912.

through personal effort on a path of initiation, and it happens naturally after death when we leave the soul world behind.

The First Three Regions

In the first region of spirit land, human beings are surrounded primarily by the spiritual archetypes of what they found on Earth, to the extent it was purely physical—minerals and plants, animals and humans, to the extent they can be imagined without life and soul. Human beings move here in the midst of thoughts that are beings; we experience directly what was only thought on Earth. Here we will feel at home if we had become familiar with the realm of the spirit: *That is me; here I meet myself.* What we have absorbed in spiritual thoughts and spiritual feelings on Earth helps us feel at home in this realm.

Here we encounter the spiritual formative forces of our own physical body; but they are no longer truly ours since, like all other things, they have become the outside world for us. We experience the spiritual archetypes of physical, bodily reality as an entity of which we were formerly part—at one time we were that ourselves! In this region we experience once more—actively in the spirit now—what belonged to our earthly life circumstances; it all comes to meet us as living thought beings. We again meet the people with whom we were connected—relatives and friends. Feelings of love and friendship rise from within and become stronger.

In this region, human beings find the foundations of spirit land—its "continental" aspect, so to speak, the part that is analogous to solid matter on Earth. The outer circumstances of our various incarnations are also part of this and are imprinted in it. But, of course, there is nothing solid or material here; however, we might think of clearly delineated forms, or hollow bodies. In the world of spirit, the spaces between (which would be empty spaces between solid bodies on Earth) are filled with differing forms related to the hollow bodies. The spiritual eye sees how, in the physical world, these hollow bodies were filled with matter, as it were, and surrounded by the continuously moving activity of the creative spiritual archetypes.

In the second region of spirit land, human beings are taken up into streaming life, the flowing movement of thought beings. They are the spiritual archetypes of life, and their region might be compared to water on Earth or, more accurately, to the blood that flows through the human body. Human beings, amid the archetypal creative forces of all that has life, recognize themselves as part of life that is no longer tied to individual life forms. Here every connection with the Earth has fallen away. Sun existence still has its aftereffects, but cosmic forces are felt more and more strongly. Here human beings find the level of communal life in which they believed but of which they had only a vague idea on Earth.

This region nourishes our religious life and feelings of worship and reverence, and here they bear fruit again. Our living religiosity enables us to experience how we form part of a harmonious, all-permeating whole. Here we are together with all those with whom we shared our ideals and with whom we practiced our religion. We join those we had found earlier because, in the realm of spirit, the spiritual regions interpenetrate. We realize that our own destiny cannot be separated from the destiny of the community to which we belong. In this region, we feel how the moral capacities with which we will enter our next life are strengthened.

All expressions of soul find their counterparts in the third region of spirit land—in a finer, more rarified element than in the first two regions. In this level, the spiritual archetypes of desires, wishes, feelings, and other soul movements form a kind of atmosphere that surrounds everything as a common world. Individual wishes, desires, and feelings of pleasure and displeasure cannot be distinguished from one another. Everything here is averse to egoism; we experience the soul movements of others as our own. Feelings, instincts, and passions determine the inner climate here. The longing of a human soul causes a soft breeze and passions a stronger gust of wind. The emotions and passions of infighting partisans appear here as storms with strong lightning and thunder claps. Here, selfless devotion and life lived in service to others bear fruit. In this region people find the capacity to serve the community. Thanks to prior lives, benefactors of humanity draw their inspiration and self-sacrificing nature in this atmosphere and are at home here. Only those who have gained a certain degree of self-knowledge free of biases are truly at home here. They are the only ones who will be able to enter the remaining regions of spirit land.

The Spirit in Spirit Land

St. Paul must have had a distinct impression of these first levels of spirit land, especially the third. He was able to speak of the suffering that creation is going through in all its members (Rom. 8:18–22). In interaction with the spiritual archetypes, which are all life and change, we human beings collaborate with them in these regions to bring change to earthly existence. Together with the beings who create the archetypes, we work on the transformation of the kingdoms of nature—the worlds of animals and plants, down to the alteration of physical forms of the Earth. Our level of spiritual development determines the length of time we participate in this joint work to create the environment that awaits us on Earth. Here we experience very clearly: *The human being is the world; the world is the human being.* In the weaving light that bathes everything on Earth we add, in our existence between death and a new birth, the effects of such deeds to all that lives on Earth.

In these first regions of spirit land the human being enters the level of cosmic spiritual life. Our inner interaction with the spiritual archetypes of everything with which we were connected on Earth takes us through successive spheres of the outer planets. In the "continental" level of spirit land, we move in the Mars sphere and in the level of the "water region" in the Jupiter sphere. In the sphere of Saturn we move in the level of the "atmosphere" of spirit land.

At the outer boundary of the Saturn sphere we have arrived at the end of what I call (for want of a better term) our "earthly cosmos." But this is not the only boundary we find in Saturn. In Saturn we come not only to the spatial boundary of this earthly cosmos, but also to a boundary that exists in time. Rudolf Steiner used the name *Saturn* for the first cosmic phase of the evolution of our solar system (see appendix 3), because the planetary Saturn sphere is the living reminder of the beginning of our world. In this Saturn, we human beings find also the level of spirit land where, on our way from incarnation to incarnation, we leave our earthly cosmos and return to it. Nonetheless, few of us enter the regions beyond the Saturn sphere consciously. Those who can sojourn there as social beings also collaborate to fructify culture on Earth. Without them, no cultural progress could exist.

This is a good moment to stop and consider that a good image for every kind of development is the picture of the planetary spheres that envelop and penetrate each other—a picture we also encounter in the levels of the soul world and the realm of the spirit. Development consists not only of stages that follow each other successively, but also means that what is coming already exists in the present, "encapsulated" in the here and now, as it were—unlike Russian matryoshka dolls, in which we find successively smaller dolls nested within larger ones. A subsequent phase of development will already be enclosed in the phase we are experiencing or examining; it is "different," but this word as such does not tell us much. The point is to discover *how* it is different.

The next levels of spirit land exemplify this. There we move into distant spaces and will have lost all direct, spatial connection with the Earth. When we embark on the path through these levels, regions of a totally different order open for us. Living into the widths of the starry world, human beings enter the actual spiritual world. Here we can sense the beginning of the fourth phase of the way, at which the human being adapts to the cosmos after death, where we can begin to work, from the outside, into the world in which we develop.

The Higher Regions

The fourth region of spirit land where human beings live next is still not the pure, absolute realm of spirit. We find no reflections in other worlds from the spiritual archetypes of this region. These living thoughts, which are living beings, have a more encompassing task. These beings, in a certain sense, form those of the lower regions into groups and give them direction. Here we find the spiritual archetypes of all that we experience in the worlds of body and soul before we actually have to deal with them. We will ourselves put creations into the world of, for example, a technical, scientific, or artistic nature; the spiritual archetypes of everything that is added to the world purely by human beings are our home in this region. Artists, scholars, inventors, and skilled politicians find their inspirations here for their contributions to culture. They are not the only ones, however. Every person finds here the source of all that transcends the everyday normal. Those who would bypass this region between death and rebirth would be unable to take any interest in what takes place outside their own little world. Since in these archetypes there is still a direct connection with what lives on Earth, in this region we have not yet reached the spirit realm *per se*.

Prior to the fifth, sixth, and seventh regions, the realms of the spirit do not differ fundamentally from previous regions. The beings who live here bestow the impulses for their activity on the archetypes of the lower regions. We find here the creative powers of the spiritual archetypes as living seeds, the objectives and goals that are the foundations of the world. When they descend to the lower regions they swell up, so to say; they expand and take on the most varied forms. The ideas with which human beings act directly in the world are reflections of those seed-like thought beings.

Those who enter these levels with open spiritual ears might become aware of a language in sounds and tones; the spiritual archetypes here *are* this language. These beings pronounce their "eternal name" not only in music, but also in word. These seed-like thought beings have an intricate nature; we could say they are composed of speech. Only their sheath has been taken from the thought world; their core comes from even higher worlds. As for human beings, our kernel of life comes from those even-higher worlds and consists of the life spirit and spirit body, which we encounter in the human seven- and ninefold being.

In the higher regions of the spirit realm, human beings learn to move in the midst of the purposes, goals, and objectives cultivated by the spirit regarding earthly life. There are no longer any reflections or dependencies here. What we are as spirit among spirits becomes clear in the fifth region of spirit land; the human spirit, freed of all possible ties to the Earth, can be completely itself. This spirit who is the identity that goes through successive incarnations and now lives fully in its own self can now freely live its own life. In this level, strengthened by the effects of deeds in prior lives, human beings add the fruits of those acts to the realm of goals and purposes.

We also create new forces here, according to how well we succeeded in the prior life in making the spirit real in thoughts, words, and deeds. Living in ourselves in this level, we live intimately with the purposes of our incarnations. Looking back on our past, we know that their aftereffects are incorporated into the purposes and intentions that form our future. A prophetic view of our next life arises in us like a flash through remembrance of our prior lives. The spirit self, which we also encountered in the seven- and ninefold human being, is at home in this level, in the reality that lives there. Human beings here find themselves amid lofty divine beings filled with divine wisdom.

In the sixth region of spirit land, we can add what transcends the necessities of our own personal destiny to our destiny. Here we accomplish what corresponds best with the true being of the world. In the seventh region of spirit land, we reach the boundary of our three worlds. We stand before the living hearts of the seed-like thought beings, among which we have moved in these last levels. At the boundary of our worlds, we come to know ourselves in the core of our own life, and the riddles of the three worlds will have been solved for us. We then become conscious of the reasons why we have chosen our specific destiny in successive lives.

We have followed the human being on the way after death from the physical world through the regions of the worlds of soul and spirit. It is an inner path, one of inner experiences that, in the end, lead human beings to their self, to the stage where they can live as spirit among spirits. We have also been able to imagine their inner experiences, which begin as a development in time and as a journey into the space of the cosmos. Thus we saw the human being move through interpenetrating planetary spheres. The soul world begins in the Moon sphere, the realm of the spirit in the Mars sphere.

Beyond the sphere of Saturn we saw the deceased in the four higher regions of spirit land beyond our earthly cosmos, moving in the widths of the world of stars, the true spirit world and the domain of the creative spiritual archetypes, the creative beings themselves. Once human beings have also learned to move at these higher levels, they will have reached the end of the three worlds that are theirs in life and death. They will have then left behind everything related to space and time, both in the physical world and in the worlds of soul and spirit.

Now, one might ask, how will I go on this path of inner experiences that takes me beyond time and space? How do human beings go this way as individuals? We have seen that this depends on the way we were able to process and work through our prior life and according to our inner disposition.

We will leave this question for now but come back to it in following chapters. For now, we still wonder whether anything actually exists beyond time and space and the three worlds.

The Godhead

When we wonder what else might exist "out there" beyond the worlds that human beings call their own—however lofty they are—the answer is: *These are the worlds of the Godhead. This is God Himself.* Throughout history, people in the most diverse cultures have imagined their gods in equally diverse ways. Some have wondered about this; we often encounter the serious and hopeful idea: *Don't we all, in the end, worship the same God?* Perhaps. It seems to me that, ultimately, the question of whom we worship is the same as the question of our capacity to travel the path that leads into the worlds of soul and spirit. The powers of worship, veneration, and serving respond to a comparable reality; we are able to worship, venerate, and serve what lies within the reach of our powers of imagination. All people really do by saying that something exceeds our power of imagination is to push something beyond them into the unknown.

Some people feel comfortable with a God of revenge; others look for their god in nature. Hinduism recognizes a trinity of the highest gods in Brahma, Shiva, and Vishnu. They are recognizable in natural phenomena; in the natural course of this world they represent the creative, destructive, and conserving principles. Then there are those who like to have their god nearby and cling to a personal god; they experience the Godhead as a divine being that is close to us. Such a personal god, we realize, is the god that is brought within the reach of our imagination by the divine being that is never far off, our own angel.

People who proclaim that they look for their god "out there" act basically in the same way. Here again, it is we who say that our god exists, depending on our capacity or incapacity to look for that god, whether nearby or far off.

We call the Godhead who dwells beyond the world where human being are able to move the Trinity, the threefold Divine as a unity. We look for this godhead on the other side of spirit land, "out there," beyond both time and space. From Him originate the plans, so to speak, for every solar system. The spirit beings we call angels, the first inhabitants of spirit land, execute these plans. The first of these angels are the Seraphim, Cherubim, and Thrones, the angels of the first hierarchy. The Kyriotetes, Dynamis, and Exusiai, the angels of the second hierarchy, and the Archai, Archangels, and Angels, those of the third hierarchy, assist them. The Trinity itself is thus much higher than the highest angels, but that is precisely where our true essence as human beings, our most individual "I," originates—beyond the sphere of the planets and beyond the zodiac of our own cosmos.

Christianity recognizes in the idea of the Trinity a godhead who is both nearby and far away, a god who is personal and is, at the same time, exalted far beyond our imagination and the experience of our own personality. "Three persons, One being," "One substance"—people in the past have tried to describe a godhead who does not one-sidedly enter our world of experience, but has more than one face. The Trinity is not just a nature god or a personal god or even imaginable. The Trinity is a triune unity, the Godhead with whom we are connected as natural human beings, the Godhead we recognize through our own free will, the Godhead who sanctifies what has fallen ill or become bad and evil. This is the Godhead we turn to with "Our

Father in heaven," whom we know stands beside us as Christ, the divine Son who is our brother. This is also the Godhead whom, in our best moments, we may just touch and whom we call Holy Spirit.

A Glimpse of Revelation

I wrote that the Trinity is the Godhead dwelling beyond the world in which human beings are able to move. Sometimes someone catches a glimpse of this godhead. This occurred for John, the Disciple whom the Lord loved, the seer who wrote down the Book of Revelation. In his second vision (Rev. 4) he saw an open door in heaven and heard a voice: "Come up here!" "Raised to the realm of the spirit," he saw a throne standing in heaven with a figure sitting on it. It is evident that John saw the heart of heaven and a throne on which sits one who is only described, not named. However, in the worship hymn of praise by the beings surrounding the throne, the one on the throne is addressed as "God the Lord, our Lord and God."

The seer describes what he observed; he described beings and phenomena, seemingly always in pairs, as if the observation of the being immediately evokes that of an activity. Thus the impression of the figure on the throne is as of two precious stones. Around the throne stands a rainbow, appearing like a third precious stone. Then the seer describes the thrones of the twenty-four elders standing around the central throne with white garments and gold crowns. Lightning flashes, voices, and thunder are heard from the throne.

Before the throne, the seven spirits of God burn as seven fiery torches; before the throne there is also something like a sea of glass or crystal. There are four living beings that give the impression of animals: "...in the midst and surrounding the throne, each with six wings, bedecked with eyes all around and within." They bring "light of the spirit, dignity of soul and thanks-offerings to Him who sits on the throne." When this happens, "the twenty-four elders bow down in worship of Him who sits on the throne" and bring in veneration the greeting of love, laying the crowns before the throne as they sing the hymn of praise.

John's descriptions give us an impression of what lies beyond the planetary spheres and worlds of the stars; the heaven of the Trinity who appears in the image of the one on the throne, who is worshipped as God and Lord, names we know from the Old Testament and the Christian tradition. He then saw a second being appearing exactly where the first being was. He saw "in the midst of the throne and the four living beings and in the midst of the elders stood a Lamb as though it had already been slain" (Rev. 5:6). The one called God has a second one beside Him, in Him. Time and again, John reached for images. He could not use concepts, because everything he saw is in continual change. Even the seemingly static picture of Him seated on the throne is full of activity. The images have to express acts, realities that in the moment are realized in color and sound.

Nowhere does our problem with this world "on the far side" become so clear as in the precious stones that are mentioned. The appearance of the one on the throne "was like jasper and carnelian." Some translators have *diamond* instead of *jasper.* In jasper, someone who is an expert sees in the mind some twenty different precious stones. "The jasper problem is not one of designation, but rather one of experience."* The experience

* Friedrich Benesch, *Apocalypse, the Transformation of Earth: An Esoteric Mineralogy*, p. 188.

of incredible hardness and clarity evokes the image of the diamond. The experience of firmness, purity, rest, and revelation leads to what is called jasper, and this experience finally leads to the heliotrope in its flaming, multicolored varieties. Benesch carefully traces all of this in his extensive study.

How can we represent the infinite riches and facets of our experience? How can the world of spirit, how can God be described? This example from the open heaven of the Revelation of John shows us how much we still have to learn to think, to feel in a different way. We get the impression that, in his descriptions, John tried to avoid any kind of fixing things in known concepts, as well as how his words in different periods of time and for different people evoke different images. When we search for our way to the spirit we would do well to base ourselves repeatedly on such a description.

Now we have reached the point when we can consider the way of the soul from a more personal point of view.

4

“Lifting up Our Eyes”

“And the rich man also died and was buried. And in the realm of shadows, where he had to endure great suffering, he lifted up his eyes...” (Luke 16:22–23). A well-known situation for someone who has immersed himself in life after death. The words are part of the old story of the rich man and poor Lazarus in the Gospel of Luke. It’s about a rich man who had a good life and who, lacking nothing, passed his days in luxury and festivities. He died and was buried. In stark contrast to this was the lot of the poor beggar Lazarus, who tried to live on the scraps that fell from the table of the rich man. “And a poor man named Lazarus lay in front of is entrance hall, covered with sores, and begged for scraps from the rich man’s table to still his hunger. And the dogs came and licked his sores.” But, when this poor Lazarus died, he was “carried by angels to Abraham’s bosom” (Luke 16:20–22).

“Abraham’s bosom” is a picture that evokes a sense of security and protection. The patriarch of the Hebrews lovingly receives poor Lazarus; Abraham was always the example whom pious believers kept before them. The story knows that our existence after death is determined by our way of life before dying. Abraham said to the rich man, “My son, remember that you had goods in your earthly life; but Lazarus only had what was bad. Now he is receiving comfort for his soul here, and you are suffering” (Luke 16:25).

The rich man, it seems, had been pushed off course by the enjoyment of his riches. He has missed the connection with the past, in which his own future lay hidden in spirit. After he is buried, when he appeals in his suffering to Abraham, the latter has to tell him that he cannot help the rich man. There is an unbridgeable chasm between their two worlds, although Abraham can still address the rich man as "my son." There is only one thing that can bridge the chasm: "They have Moses and the prophets; let them listen to them" (Luke 16:29). In our language, this means that during our life we must never ignore or neglect the personal moral dimension.

The story also shows that after death a settlement takes place. The consequences of the way we have lived are of a moral nature. In a previous chapter we saw that life in the body causes problems once death has come. Rudolf Steiner spoke of certain feelings of warmth and cold with which human beings struggle in the soul world (chapter 2). It is difficult for all of us to adapt quickly. Finding that we can no longer express ourselves evokes warmth; finding that we can no longer act evokes cold. Those who have lived materialistic lives will experience such torments correspondingly more strongly.

The degree to which we must fight against the condition in which our soul then lives depends on the extent to which we have devoted ourselves to the good things we received during our life. The New Testament never stops emphasizing this; it speaks, too, about the need to know where we stand in our inner life—whether we desire to serve God or the god of money, Mammon. Entering that other way of existence, the realm of the heavens, is no simple matter for those who got caught up in earthly baubles and trinkets. "A camel will more easily go through the eye of a needle than a rich man will enter the kingdom of God" (Matt. 19:24). This is a very clear picture. A rich man is simply too big, too fat; his riches have made him swell up, and he has lost the flexibility needed to move around. It is cheery, therefore, that there are those who find a new orientation and let go of what ties them down, such as Zaccheus, the tax collector who, in another story, promised to make restitution during his earthly life (Luke 19:1–10).

The fact that we cannot instantly make a huge change when this is asked of us after our funeral is demonstrated by a more modern version of the story of the rich man and the beggar, which uses the well-known pictures of heaven and hell. The rich man, says the story, is received at the gates of heaven by Peter, who tells everyone that they may say how they would like things around them to be. The rich man wants to be rich in heaven, too, with a golden castle and cellars full of money. He even knows exactly what he wants to eat. He expects a comfortable chair, and the daily paper must not be forgotten.

After quite a few years the man starts to feel bored. He sits alone in his room, no one talks to him; one day is exactly like the one before; the world he reads about in the newspaper has become alien to him. He complains bitterly when Peter drops by to ask him how he is doing. "Your heaven with its eternal bliss—what a pitiful business!" "Heaven?" says Peter, "What do you mean 'heaven'? You don't think you are in heaven, do you? You yourself wanted to be in hell!" For the rich man it is a new idea that hell has been modernized and that you no longer have to expect devils and cauldrons. He begins to understand that, if life after death is a continuation of life on Earth, it will be dreadfully dull, and with this he finds the beginning of a turnabout.

The story of the rich man and poor Lazarus has a kind of precursor in the parable of the rich farmer whose land produced such a good harvest that he no longer had enough space to store it all. Thus he decides to tear down his barns and build new ones. He relishes the prospect: "I shall say to my soul: My soul, now you have many goods stored up, which will last for many years; be at ease, eat, drink, be merry. But God spoke to him: You fool! This very night they will demand your life; and the things you have collected, whose will they be?" This story is a warning to "everyone who lays up earthly goods for himself but has no riches which endure before God" (Luke 12:19–21).

In the stories about these rich people, the personal note sounds that we are looking for in this chapter. Speaking biblically, is "my soul" rich in earthly goods that were collected for its use alone? Is it completely self-absorbed? Or is it "rich in God" and open to God and His worlds? In other words, can my soul communicate with the soul world and the spirit world, the realms of the Triune God, or is it caught up in itself? Will it succeed in looking up, in "lifting up its eyes?" Do the torments help to open the eyes of the soul?

First Sensations

Once we have died, at first we can only briefly "lift up our eyes." This moment is part of a slow, gradual process that will enable us to "keep our eyes open" in that other world. For some people it may take months, even years, before they are able to do this. The first "awaking" sometimes happens as the heat of the cremation envelops the body, as Rudolf Steiner once related.* We have sensations from the beginning, but these relate at first only to what we have left behind.

---

* Rudolf Steiner, *Das Geheimnis des Todes*, Mar. 7, 1915.

After dying our first overwhelming impression is that of the body we left behind. We see it then for the first time truly from the outside, and we know, *From now on, I am aware of myself without this body; I can now go on without this body.* This awareness stays with us, and again and again we will evoke our consciousness of self, our "I"-consciousness, when we look back at the moment of dying. The retrospect of having died makes us creative, and because of this we also no longer depend on an existence that was bestowed on us. We continuously create ourselves anew, as it were, when we fall back on the moment of our death.

Our entire existence after death rests on such continual activity. When we sleep and are outside our body during life, there is always a craving to reenter the body. Now that this craving for the body has to fall away, remembrance and awareness of the body take its place. The body we have left behind disintegrates into its constituent parts and awakes awareness of ourselves as an "I," and by the grace of this awareness of the physical body we maintain our connection with life on Earth.

The second overwhelming sensation is that we now also see the Earth on which we lived from outside. From outside, we see everything that became the content of our consciousness. This has shrunk to a shining star. From this fiery, pulsing, reddish star shines the memory tableau of our life. We sense the body that becomes part of the Earth, which we have abandoned, is pure will; it's as though it were a star consisting completely of will. In the widths, where we are now moving, our life shines to us in a great tableau in the fiery glow of this will. In this experience of our inner being, now far outside us, our powers of consciousness awake.

We understand that we do not immediately acquire the consciousness we need for life after death. It is a difficult process of adjusting, especially in regard to the power of the consciousness with which we enter this new world after letting go of our etheric body; we have much too much consciousness. We are so filled with power of consciousness that it blinds us; we are overcome by it as if by a kind of sleep. To awake to the world of spirit, our consciousness has to be dimmed until it comes into harmony with the powers we acquired during life. Thus we limit ourselves at first to looking back on the life just ended and gaining self-knowledge from it. This mitigates our consciousness, so that we gradually learn to tolerate and wake up to the world of spirit.

Affinity

One aspect of the torments was discussed in the description of the first regions of the soul world, where the attraction of earthly life still works in the confrontation with overwhelming soul forms of sympathy and antipathy. Every human being will experience the falling away of the physical organs as a feeling of burning thirst, a completely disabling heat. By contrast, we feel something like an icy, rigidifying feeling rise in us once the will can no longer express itself. According to the way we have lived, we are thus more or less receptive to the one-sidedness with which sympathy and antipathy are present here, and our time of detachment will take longer or shorter.

At the beginning, the difficulties of the soul to experience its sojourn in the hereafter in a good way is nicely illustrated by the story of the rich man who is allowed to express his wishes to Peter at the gate of heaven. He just knows that he can continue his life as he had lived it before, and that all his wishes and needs will be met as they were before he died.

We are stuck in the first regions of the soul world for as long as we have an affinity with them. Desires, illusions, wishes—every aspect of our desires for gratification—keep the soul imprisoned until it no longer feels a burning longing for sensory pleasure and for the way of thinking it was accustomed to. It lasts until the soul becomes perfectly happy with no desire to pull it down to the sub-lunar world.

Sub-lunar indeed; the three lower regions of the soul world are, as we have seen, part of the Moon sphere. During the time when we remain in the process of outgrowing our life on Earth we remain close to the Earth. Once we have sufficiently progressed in our purification, we move on to the fourth soul region, that of pleasure and displeasure, where we also become aware of the fact that purification, despite the pains of detachment, is not solely suffering. Gradually, our longing for purification grows, because we cannot take the next step on the path until our imperfections fall away. We are fettered to these regions until we have overcome our every last longing and the soul can enter the Mercury sphere.

Fortunately, during life on Earth we are not a hundred percent caught up in our own desires. We are not always jealous of others and do not always insist on getting and consuming everything for ourselves. In the economic sphere of life especially, we begin to practice give and take and sharing, whereby we experience something like brotherhood. We can take this quietly into death, as something we can develop there, particularly because something like this does not need to be endlessly talked about but can simply be done.

Physiognomy

Another aspect of these torments has to do with our intimate connection with the whole cosmos. Rudolf Steiner's work includes the idea that human beings as microcosm express the macrocosm, the great wide cosmos. For instance, in one of his aphorisms Steiner said: "Know yourself, and you find the secrets of the world. Behold the world, and you find the secrets of your own being." And:

> If we fully know our self,
> our self becomes the world;
> if we fully know the world,
> the world becomes our self.*

We are familiar with a similar phenomenon in our daily life; our face can express our being, fleeting moods, or certain characteristics. Indeed, our entire form can express a soul condition that has become dominant. Stage actors use this: "miser," "professor," and so on, are expressed on the stage when their characteristics are emphasized in a one-sided way. Although an interest in physiognomy can degenerate into stereotypes, it is an art to understand people through their facial expressions and physical constitution. Rudolf Steiner used these experiences to describe what happens to the soul after death.

We have seen how the soul can get stuck in certain lower spheres of the soul world, depending on whether it is akin or has a certain similarity to them. In a lecture series in 1923, Steiner used the concept of physiognomy** to show how the soul expands in the planetary spheres during its time of purification.*** Even in the case of the deceased described there, we can still speak of a figure, or form, and as with a living person that form expresses the soul–spiritual being of the deceased.

---

* Rudolf Steiner, *Truth-Wrought-Words*, p. 71 (trans. revised by P.M.).

** The word *physiognomy* is used in the sense of "outer expression of inner essence."

*** Rudolf Steiner, *At Home in the Universe*, Nov. 1923.

Once the deceased have successively given up the material body and etheric body, a spirit figure frees itself from those sheaths. At first, this figure resembles the physical form, but it goes through continuous transformations until it becomes all "physiognomy," a complete expression of its inner life. Through this, those who have died come to express their moral spiritual entity, both good and bad. It's not that something like an earthly face appears; that fades away. Rather, other parts of the figure develop a distinct physiognomy. The chest and lungs, for example, show whether we were cowardly or courageous during life, and whether we were willing to go for it or had the tendency to cede our place. The arms and hands become highly expressive after death, even to the point that the life story of the person can be read in them. If we want to describe such a spirit figure, said Rudolf Steiner, we have to use images that we are used to.* However, we must also bear in mind that such descriptions are always mere aids; no one can ever describe, for instance, the size of such appearances.

In this spirit figure of the human being, the part that was our head gradually fades. The rest of the figure, however, becomes all physiognomy that bluntly expresses, one could say, how we have become during our life. We have left our earthly way of thinking behind. Of what use would it be anyway, since we no longer have a head? Our soul life increasingly consists of picturing images—viewing picturing, from which thoughts reveal themselves as everything we are aware of in our surroundings. During life on Earth, we produce our thoughts; after death they appear as expressions of spiritual entities, but we encounter one surprise after another. Consider, for instance, the stars or the Moon.

* Ibid., Nov. 17, 1923.

In the Sphere of the Moon

During life we see only the outer stars and planets, shining from far distances; although, under certain conditions, they seem to be so near that it seems we could pluck them from the sky. After death they appear as colonies of spiritual beings, distinctly different from one another. The Moon, which we consider among the planets spiritually freed itself from the Earth over the course of time. Once independent, it became a dwelling of spiritual beings—specifically, those who guided humanity in the very far distant past, primeval teachers of humanity who stand higher and are greater than we are as humans. "Greater" in the sense of John the Baptist who, in the words of the Gospel of Matthew, is yet smaller than the smallest in the Kingdom of Heaven (Matt. 11:11). These are beings between human beings and the angels. In an outer sense, the Moon reflects the light of the Sun, whereas inwardly it reflects cosmic forces related to what is subhuman and animalistic in us.

In the Moon sphere, with these great contrasts, the deceased have their first experiences, depending on their moral or immoral physiognomy. When we "lift up our eyes" there, we do not actually see with our eyes; it is indeed a kind of viewing but more in the form of a sensation that is also experiencing and, in a certain sense, a sort of feeling at a distance. Nonetheless, we become immediately aware of the boundaries posed by our own spiritual form, for we are still completely enclosed in our own soul nature and caught in our wishes and interests. We live in complete ignorance of other souls there with a different morality, even though all the dead merge into one another's physiognomic "skins." We interpenetrate in this way, but we are aware of only like-minded souls.

We are mobile and soft in our own physiognomy. When we notice another being nearby, we try to become like it, but we cannot change; we are still as we were on Earth. Living among these other souls, we can feel profoundly alone. Real criminals, for example, are unable to adopt the physiognomy of a good person; they can dwell only among the like-minded souls of other criminals. During the first period after death, we are impelled therefore to move exclusively among other souls who are similar to us morally. Thus we receive a strong first impression that is also a stern and absolute judgment. We know: *Just as they are there, I am as well!* In the Moon sphere we begin to get an idea of all that is on our karmic record.

In the vicinity of the Moon, angels cannot remain close to someone who recently died, for then we are still too burdened by all that keeps us in proximity to the Earth. We are still dragging along with us our feelings of self-worth and feelings acquired as a result of our social position. Our self-image that we hoped to see reflected in the eyes of others still burdens us, as do the concerns we had to leave behind, things we left unfinished.

During this first period, the protest that Christian Morgenstern formulated about earthly humanity still applies to all of us: "Must I descend with you into your worlds, from which the horror of corruption breathes, plunge with you to the kingdom of the dead..."* Evil spirits dwell in that region. The deceased who find themselves in the company of souls with physiognomies that are not very attractive discover to their despair that they recognize those evil spirits in those souls. This second impression, or judgment, lets them know the degree to which they have become similar to the evil spirits. This is another shock that works as a stern judgment.

* Christian Morgenstern, *We Have Found a Path*, p. 85 (trans. by P.M.).

The third powerful impression is that of the primeval teachers of humanity. The evil spirits always hope to draw these primeval teachers into their orbit. They hope to make the dead who have reprehensible physiognomies known to the primeval teachers because they want to hold the world at a certain point of development. In this way, they reveal themselves as spirits who serve Ahriman (see appendix 6). They want people to remain at the point they have reached and to live in the luster of the past.

Without the wisdom of the primeval teachers, human development on Earth would not have begun; on the other hand, human beings would not have progressed if the primeval wisdom had remained with them forever. Their wisdom spoke to our instincts not to the thinking of free human beings; at a certain point, in order to leave human beings free, the primeval teachers withdrew to the Moon. This is the third impression for those who do not express a physiognomy of the good: *I cannot see any of those who are supposed to be here, from whom we human beings received our origin; I feel repulsed, abandoned!*

Insight into Destiny

In order to grow toward the Mercury sphere, during the final part of our sojourn in the Moon sphere we will have to overcome the gravitational pull of the sub-lunar world. Once we have completed our physiognomy, expressing our moral spiritual condition, we begin to encounter souls with whom we share a destiny, with whom we have had a spiritual connection of heart or feeling. We come to know one another completely; no one need tell another anything.

At this time we also come to know the spiritual beings of the third hierarchy: Angels, Archangels, and Archai. Our encounters with them depend on our own nature, for they always have a pure physiognomy; they do not hide anything of their spiritual appearance but are all physiognomy. Observing them is always a resplendent moment, under the gaze of those who are nearby and can no longer hide. The souls with whom we share no destiny simply do not exist for us; they move outside the sphere for which we can generate interest. Thus we learn of those who are close to us, and we experience how the angels receive them with greater or lesser joy. Then the time comes when we leave, as it were, the memories in which we have lived and that have become transparent to us.

After dying, we all receive such impressions, some more than others. However, the more we can appear in the physiognomy of the good, the more frequently we will perceive beings to whom we will have become similar through the good. What arises from ahrimanic beings will fall away, and our sense organ for perceiving the angels becomes more acute. We will receive strength from them—first of all, strength of will. After death, the will replaces thinking; the will becomes sensation, perception, the sense organ that opens the world in which we then live. We cannot make it without the will; only through the will can we become alike to what we want to observe. After all, every impression mentioned works on the will.

The next sphere that the deceased enter is that of Mercury, formed by the visible planet Venus (see chapter 2). Here, in the region of soul light, the actual soul world opens to us. By then, we will have shed the physiognomy of evil, often through great pain. We will have become a little more like the Angels, Archangels, and Archai; for many of the dead, however, this requires a long time. Our morality continues to set up boundaries for us; and we gradually have to learn to break down our walls.

In this sphere, too, souls still completely penetrate one another; here, too, our morality determines those with whom we can come into contact, as well as whether we can discover the others with whom we share this sphere. We are still bound by the facts we created during earthly life; we cannot change them now, and we suffer from our incapacity to change anything. In our suffering, the will awakes to do something about this later; the will awakes to compensate, for this is how destiny operates.

We develop understanding for everything that during life was initially only a movement of the will that lived in us more or less invisibly. Now we also begin to observe with greater understanding all those who share our destiny. We come to understand one another better in a spiritual sense and to develop insight into what the spiritual, moral physiognomies surrounding us mean for one another. We develop insight into destiny and see how destiny connections determine the future for everyone. We begin to understand how such a destiny will go in the future.

Hermit or Social Being

In the Mercury sphere it becomes clear that those who rejected spiritual matters during earthly life and drenched themselves in materialism can generate little understanding of the beings of this realm. A confirmed materialist will also have a hard time in the sphere of Venus, formed by the physical planet Mercury. Here we meet the spiritual beings of the third hierarchy, who are already more advanced in their development. Forces of cosmic love irradiate us in this region of active soul power. Those who did not learn to love on Earth will experience this love as its opposite: wrath. If we have brought a lot of hatred with us from our life on Earth, here we will feel wrath and rage rise in our own will. Then we realize: *This rage has to be restrained; it has to brought into harmony with the realities of this soul region.*

In this region we begin to grow together with our companions in destiny and begin to orient ourselves toward a common future. We feel we are taken up by the spirit of the planets' movements, the spirit of the forces of the planetary system. Along with our destiny companions, this brings us into the vicinity of the spiritual Sun existence.

Thus we become increasingly like the beings in the spiritual cosmos. All the while, it is the will that truly counts in these regions; the will in particular must be developed. Our whole physiognomy receives its form from the will, which lives in the limbs and metabolism of earthly human beings. We notice that our head, which was so prominent on Earth, has gradually disappeared and dissolved into a kind of spiritual mist. Even in the sphere of Mercury, thoughts retain a certain significance, but in the Venus sphere love replaces wisdom, so to speak.

Looking back, we can say that, according to our soul's moral content, in the Mercury sphere we become either companionable, social souls or hermits who are unable to free ourselves from the mists of our own views. In the sphere of Venus, the soul's religious disposition is decisively important. Without a religious inclination, regardless of how it might have been practiced on Earth, we cannot easily escape spiritual narrow-mindedness; it's as if we want to hide in our own little house. Also all those who were stuck in the limitations of their own ideas on faith remain as captives, caught in their own little cages.

We become truly social beings in this sphere only through all-encompassing religiosity, through a fundamental religious disposition of the soul that connects us with the divine powers who are the ground of existence and all that lives. It is a disposition that allows us to say with Paul, as he spoke of the God who was still an unknown entity to the Athenians: "For in Him we live and move and have our being" (Acts 17:28). Thus, in this region of active soul power, we also find the forces we need to receive a reasonable astral body for our next life.

In this chapter we have seen how after death we gradually "lift up our eyes," the forms this takes, and how the soul makes itself at home in its world. At the stage when this takes place, the soul is still in the soul world and on the way to the Sun sphere. But before we follow the soul further, I want to add a few other aspects.

5

What Is the Human Being?

What is the human being? This is a question that might sound like a lamentation, or it might be asked with a shrug. What is this human being who cooks up catastrophe after catastrophe among fellow human beings and who appears to go out of the way to make Earth unlivable; one who is also capable of unexpected acts of altruism—the speck of dust in the universe that will soon be cloned?

Human beings—we are bearers of the spirit. Some people recognize in our word *man* an Indo–Germanic word that indicates thinking. For those who are familiar with Greek, *man* can be someone who looks upward: *anthropos*. For people who know Latin, *man* is related to the Earth—*homo,* in whose humanity the earthly element, *humus*, is present.

The same idea sounds in the common Hebrew word for human being, *adam*, the word we know as the name of the first human being described in Genesis 2. The earthly aspect implied in these languages has become predominant today, to the point that the spiritual aspect has almost completely disappeared. Human beings who lift up their eyes, who look upward, and who are bearers of the spirit barely count anymore.

We also realize that, when we try to answer this question, we can become easily caught up in clichés. Our thoughts run all too eagerly along firm, well-traveled paths; we connect thoughts with one another because others have done it before us, or because we saw something in the news or on TV. Most of the thoughts that play through our head are no more than projections of language, so to speak, words that clot together in stereotypical connections.

What is all too often missing is the *will to think,* the sensation of the will we can experience when we have the tiller of our thinking firmly in hand—the perception of what is active in the thoughts, the arbitrary, the capricious aspect that does not choose well-traveled paths. The question of what is a human being receives the right dimension when it is asked as a religious question, as in Psalm 8:4: "What are mere mortals that you should be mindful of them, human beings that you should care for them?" The question is asked under the heavens that speak of the creative work of the Godhead.

What, then, is this human being, this transitory, perishable being, this "mortal?" For the psalmist uses this word in his question, not the word that views the human being as fashioned from the soil. But he does not stop with the question of the human as a mortal being, whom God holds in His mind and who is carried in God's consciousness. The question is not complete until it is also asked of the future human being, the "son of man" who, as the son of "adam," is connected with the Earth, without the overtone of the perishable.

As Rudolf Frieling said in his discussion of this Psalm,* the son of man is the future-oriented human being who grows toward new possibilities. It is the figure who, from the old human being marked by the Fall into sin and by death, will emerge as new and harbors forces that can unfold in the future. In Christ, this son of man has vanquished mortality and death and set an example for all humankind of the resurrection of the human being.

* Rudolf Frieling, *Hidden Treasures in the Psalms*, pp. 11ff.

Rudolf Frieling also called attention to how, in the polarity of "being mindful of" and "care for" human beings, the elements of thinking and will stand side by side. God "is mindful" of mortal humankind; He carries us in his consciousness. He "cares for" the son of Adam and offers His real help.

In life after death, the question of what is the human being stands before us in all its drama, in our own life and in that of others. But to understand the answers we get to hear there, nothing with the slightest tendency toward the earthly ways of thinking helps at all.

The Sphere of the Sun

In the first part of the way through the soul world, principally a way of detaching, the soul loses the craving for thoughts bound to the physical body. This happens in the region of flowing sensitivity, the second soul region. We gradually begin to think differently from the way we do on Earth. Our soul life becomes a beholding in pictures, and we begin to be open to the kind of thoughts that are not our own products but expressions of spiritual beings. Even when we are in the fifth soul region, or sphere of Mercury, thoughts have some significance, albeit in a metamorphosed form. The will then begins to be perceptive power; the soul becomes all activity.

Viewed cosmically, the region of soul life, the seventh and last region of the soul world, is the sphere of the Sun. At the end of its purification phase, the soul enters its true element, and we will no longer lose the radiance of Sun existence once we feel at home in the world of spirit in the subsequent planetary spheres. However, to really thrive in the Sun sphere we have to develop understanding for *all* people, not just for a certain limited group with whom we feel comfortable. Those who still have something in their soul that reeks of the sort of prejudice that "the true churches" love to plant in the hearts of their followers will live here as loners, separated from all others. Being separated in this way and lacking understanding for others become sources of terrible suffering for those who have grown into the Sun sphere together with others to fully penetrate into one another. Interpenetrating each other, we experience encounters with others who believed something we could not acknowledge as a continuous reproach against us, for we are unable to meet that human being.

This must not always have been so. In pre-Christian times, we could be one-sided. Only the great leaders, the priests and kings, had to learn to bridge all earthly differences through understanding. This is what Abraham underwent after a decisive moment in his life when he met Melchizedek, the king of Salem, at the place where the temple was later built by Solomon. Melchizedek was also a priest of God Most High, for whom no one-sidedness can stand.

Today, the crucial test is whether we have the deep conviction of Paul, that Christ brought the light of the resurrection of the dead to the Jews as well as to the pagans. For true comprehension of Christ, no Christianity is decisive that continues pre-Christian experiences of religions in the myriad of different forms of Christian faith. What counts today is whether people can be awakened in their soul through the power of the Resurrection—in other words, whether we have caught some of the light that shines from the resurrected Christ. This enables us to recognize the purely human in others and to interact with them on that basis.

Those who have been able to catch a glimpse of the reality of Christ in this way will have contact with others in Sun existence. This is supremely important, because we now experience a decisive moment in our whole humanness. For, now we begin to hear continuously the words: *You are a god; you will be a god.* With seductive power, this sounds from the mouth of Lucifer, the spirit of light who works on the Earth as the *diabolos,* the "accuser," the slanderer who sows confusion in everything. He is the one who, as the serpent, told the woman in paradise: "You will be like God, knowing good and evil" (Gen. 3:5).

According to Rudolf Steiner, in the Sun sphere, superficially speaking, we see two thrones. From the first throne, which is never empty, we hear Lucifer speak. He sits there in all his seductive glory. The other throne, the one of Christ, appears empty to many people, because we cannot perceive him unless we have deepened our understanding of Christ during our life on Earth. Then we experience the right dimension of "You are gods." Then our eyes are opened for the Christ as "the spirit who, bestowing grace, wends throughout the world-all being," in the words of a meditative verse Rudolf Steiner wrote on his sickbed in November 1924:*

> Sun, you radiance harborer,
> your pure light's material power
> conjures life from out of the Earth's
> immeasurably fertile deeps.
>
> Heart, you soul-source harborer,
> your warm light's bright spirit power
> conjures life from humankind's own
> immeasurably deep inmost.

* Rudolf Steiner, *Truth-Wrought-Words* (trans. revised by P.M.), p. 63.

When I gaze into the Sun,
radiantly it speaks to me
of the spirit who, grace-giving,
wends through the world-all being.

When I feel into my heart,
the spirit speaks its own true word—
speaks of the human, whom it loves
through time and all eternity.

I can see, when I look upward
deep into the Sun's bright orb,
the world's great glowing heart.

I can feel when I look inward
deep into the heart's warm beat,
the soul-bright human sun.

Christ

Those who have drawn forces from the Sun sphere—religious forces—during life on Earth are well prepared for what awaits them there, especially if we have developed an understanding of the Christ mystery. The death and resurrection of Christ have been decisive for this mystery; His activity in the Sun sphere belongs to all times. In pre-Christian times, Abraham, for example, was able to obtain the forces he would need in the Sun sphere through his meeting with Melchizedek. Through the death and resurrection of Christ, the Christ mystery has become a critical factor in the development of all humanity; the gift of the Christ mystery exists for all human beings. Each of us has to draw the forces we need from the Sun sphere so that on the way back to Earth, during our preparation for the next life, we can obtain our etheric body in the right way.

After death, we take what we have received in the Sun sphere with us when we begin to live in the spheres of the outer planets. When we enter the Sun sphere, the soul is not yet free of all that took place in our past life. The soul has to come to a state of peace regarding all that transcends the strictly personal, its morality, its religiosity, and its humanity. Until then we are not free to enter cosmic spiritual life.

Regardless of our relationship to Christ during life, in death he helps us make the transition from mortal human to future human being. He created the potential for this after his death on the cross, when he opened the future again for the soul. As time progressed before Christ's coming, more and more people felt that after death they were stuck, so to speak, in the lower regions of the soul world. Legends speak of this, as do ancient Easter plays; they show us how the shackles of the soul were broken when Christ went into the underworld on Holy Saturday to bring the light of the Resurrection. After the first resurrection in the soul world, the second resurrection followed on Easter Sunday—resurrection from the grave of the Earth, which annulled bodily death. For the present, the victory over the death of the body is for us as human beings still a goal that lies in the far distant future. When we awake to the soul world after death, however, we can, we must, experience in soul the victory over death in the soul in order to be able to continue existence as spiritual beings.

Before we begin to relive our life in reverse in kamaloka, we experience two spiritual figures standing before us. One holds up a kind of list of all that had the stain of selfishness in our life. Most people who are part of Western culture recognize Moses in this figure, holding a record of their sins. He holds up the "Tablets of the Law" and asks for accountability for what we have on our karmic record, the record of our destiny. When he does this, we know with great precision where we deviated from the Law.

The second figure facing us is that of the Cherub with the "flaming sword that turned every way," who was first seen when Adam and Eve were expelled from Paradise (Gen. 3:24). He passes judgment on everything whereby we deviated from the right path. In this way, our karmic account is made up. Today, the figure of Moses, who has increasingly connected himself with Christ, is undergoing a transformation. As people connect themselves with the living, suprasensory Christ, the figure of Moses is transformed for them into that of Christ. Thus Christ becomes part of our destiny. He becomes the Lord of karma.

The Burden of Destiny

When Christ becomes the Lord of destiny, the balancing, reconciliation of karma also gains a different character. This will no longer occur just for us, but also for the whole community of human beings. For this reason, the settlement we prepare because of our deeds will also be able to become a blessing for our environment. This becomes possible because Christ has removed part of the burden of our destiny. In the picture of the Gospels, He is the "Lamb of God who takes the sin of the world upon himself" (John 1:29). Mark well "the sin of the world," for we can sense repeatedly that our actions not only have consequences for ourselves but also stand as facts in the world and have consequences for others.

The load of guilt we carry and for which we have to atone has a personal aspect for our own destiny, as well as an aspect that affects the world as such and transcends the personal. The personal aspect of our guilt becomes a part of what we have to do to correct our destiny. Whatever transcends the personal exceeds our capacity to do this. Consequently, Christ has taken this on Himself. Because of this, the Earth is no longer burdened by all that guilt and has become free to develop along with us humans. Therefore, the words spoken by Christ, "Your sins are forgiven," do not express a karmic fact but rather a *cosmic fact.* In our destiny we will have to live with the consequences of our own deeds, but Christ takes on Himself what exceeds our powers. The following story gives a picture of this reality.

> A boy grew up in a large, beautiful house. He could go anywhere, but there was a door to one room that was always locked. When he had nearly grown up, he asked his parents, "Why is that door always locked? Let me see what's behind it." He was given the key, and after he opened the door he saw that the back of the door was full of nails, large ones and small ones, and there were also some nail holes. He was startled and asked his parents why the door was so damaged. "This is your door," he was told. "Every time you did something that wasn't satisfactory, a nail was added, sometimes a large one and sometimes a small one, depending on what you had done wrong. Whenever you did something good, a nail could be pulled out." He understood that good deeds counterbalance bad ones, but he was truly startled when he realized that the nail holes could not be removed by this method of counterbalancing.

With this picture of the damaged door we can say: *We must leave it to Christ to fill in the holes that remain after we have been allowed to use the world as a practice ground for our destiny.*

The Spiritual Sun

Sun existence throws its rays ahead into the future. Before Christ became the Lord of destiny he had already shown pity on us in other ways so as to heal the rupture caused by death. Let's consider two examples of this.

During our life on Earth, we always experience ourselves as "me" through the constant confrontation with the outside world through our senses. When we wake each morning—after our sojourn in the world that hides behind that of the senses, this wondrous, centripetal world—we have our meeting with the body we left behind when we fell asleep. During life we owe our "I"-consciousness to this kind of confrontation. When the body falls away at death, and with it our contact with the world behind the senses, our "I"-consciousness awakes in another way. This happens because, during the whole time between death and a new birth, we can look back on the moment of dying. When we do so, we are aware each time of the spirit power that creatively self-generates. This experience is the foundation of our "I"-consciousness in the world of spirit. Without the life that Christ wrested from the hands of death, we would be unable to experience this. He bestows the power on us to be able to look back and the power to take the remembrance of having died with us, so long as it is needed.

Subsequently, when the etheric body begins to dissolve into the world of the etheric, we can observe two opposite elements in it that remind us of what we knew on Earth. On the one hand, we find the forces of our physical demise there, the forces of death that await all matter. These forces carry the seed of decomposition in them and point to all that will disintegrate and fall apart. Thus we find potential death in our etheric body, but also potential life.

We also observe forces in it that remind us of the seeds of plants, forces that guarantee continued existence and growth. These are young forces that embody the future; they are permeated by the power of Christ. But we do not become aware of this germinating part of our etheric body unless we have a relationship with the Christ mystery, which is now open to us in our development. In this way we become aware of how our future is assured in Christ; we meet Him again in Sun existence, the sphere of the Sun. Through Him we have acquired the inner kinship with the Sun that bestows the forces for another life on our etheric body.

We spend the largest part of our time between death and a new birth in the Sun sphere, the spiritual essence of the Sun. It is the dwelling place of the angels of the second heavenly hierarchy, the Exousiai, Dynamis, and Kyriotetes, who are, so to speak, the soul and spirit of the Sun's life. These angelic powers live immeasurably far above everything that makes us, as human beings, earthly creatures. There are of course no laws of nature in the life of the Sun, as there are on Earth; there, spiritual, moral law and natural law are one and the same.

On Earth, the discrepancy between the two leads to remarkable situations. We can try to lead a reasonably good life based on our morally good views, and we might be able to observe bad intentions in others once in a while. It may happen then that, despite all our good will and efforts, things are not going well for us in material terms; we might even be doing quite poorly, whereas we see that someone else, who has objectionable intentions, is doing just fine. "That God allows it..." someone might then say. However, there is nothing God can do about it, because He refrains from intervening arbitrarily in His creation. He has accepted the abyss between "inside" and "outside," between inner spiritual intentions and earthly material realities. He is actually forced to suffer this discrepancy, and He could break through it only by causing chaos in His own creation. Therefore, if we want to know the tree for its fruits, we should look not only at the pretty skin of the fruit, but also examine whether it might be rotten inside.

In this Sun existence, everything happens in accordance with spiritual laws. Here it is possible to bring intentions to realization that we were never able to realize on Earth. Here good intentions have effects according to their power of good, and evil intentions according to the power of their evil. What counts is not our good or bad nature but the power present in our nature. Everything good that human beings have experienced in their soul is sympathetically absorbed during Sun existence, but all that is bad that the soul brings with it is rejected. Of course, the Sun shines on all people, the good and the bad, but the latter have no access to Sun life, whereas the former will—in the words of the Bible, "Shine like the Sun." They will have become of the same nature as Sun existence.

In the Sun Sphere

This can, however, lead to problems. Take, for instance, a true criminal, evil through and through. Such individuals have great difficulties in kamaloka and go through the spheres of Moon, Mercury, and Venus the best way they can, but at Sun existence they have to give up. They simply have no access there and are soundly rejected. They have nothing in common with the Sun. All they can do is turn around and go back in the direction of a subsequent life. Real criminals will reappear on Earth very soon after death. Others have to leave behind everything that does not agree with Sun life before entering that sphere. Later, on their way to the next life, they will pick it up again.

On our way toward Sun existence, while we are in the Moon sphere we give up everything in us that is morally useless for the cosmos. We leave the Moon sphere as a human being with no deleterious moral effect on the cosmos, In the sphere of Mercury, we will also give up the spiritual counterpart of our ailments, along with everything that they caused in us. We become healthy in our soul. We can become so healthy there that we no longer pose a problem to the realms of the spiritual spheres—at least in the sense that we no longer need to be isolated in the spiritual environment because of our condition.

After some tens of year, no longer radiating moral or mental–physical weaknesses, we enter the Venus sphere where we will be further prepared to go into Sun existence. But in this situation, we will no longer be able to remain a complete person. On Earth, our moral weakness can be veiled; diseases can remain hidden. Because every weakness, viewed spiritually, is a part of who we are—no less real than the causes and consequences of our physical illnesses—we arrive in the Venus sphere badly damaged. Fortunately, Venus is pure love in a spiritual sense, and this cosmic love will carry what is left of us into Sun existence.

Then we go to work in Sun existence; we begin to prepare our destiny for the next life. Where are we at that point—in the sphere of the Sun, a so-called ball of burning gasses? According to Rudolf Steiner this picture is completely wrong.* What is the Sun really like, then?

Think of a bottle of soda water. You don't actually see the water, but you can see the bubbles as they rise because they are

---

* Rudolf Steiner, *Karmic Relationships*, vol. 7, p. 25.

lighter than the water. Water is denser and heavier; gas is thinner and lighter. The same is true of our perception of the Sun, said Steiner. We see the Sun because space is more rarefied there. But isn't space already nothing? Indeed, but where the Sun is there is even less than nothing. Where the Sun is, there is a hole in space, as it were, and the angels of the second hierarchy, the Exousiai, Dynamis, and Kyriotetes live in the space of this hole.

As human beings, we spend most of our time between death and rebirth there with these angels, together with those who have died, with whom we have a karmic connection. We work with them on our further destiny. Within that hole in space—this less than nothing—we find the pure spiritual world where laws help develop karmic consequences from the good that the many souls bring into it. Those laws also help heal injuries caused by bad karma.

Here, at first, we prepare especially the physical constitution of our next life and later, let's say, the moral–spiritual part of our destiny together with the angels of the second hierarchy. In the Sun sphere, during the two preparatory stages for the next incarnation, the question of what is a human being receives a concrete answer. From an earthly perspective, we might wonder what is perishable in us and what has eternal value. From the perspective of the Sun, we receive an answer that consists of the preparation of our future constitution and coming destiny.

Let's stop here. To those who would like to become more familiar with the spiritual sun described here, I recommend Georg Blattmann's book *The Sun.**

In the following chapters we will examine more closely certain aspects of our path toward and within this Sun existence.

* See Georg Blattmann, *The Sun: The Ancient Mysteries and the New Physics.*

6

Reversal: Inside Turns Out

Being "turned inside out" is a fundamental experience in the transition from life to death and from death to life. Inside becomes outside; outside becomes inside. In our cosmic past as human beings, we were once turned inside out for the first time. What was formed as our body in earlier cosmic eras was then turned inside out, as we can do with a glove. What had been prepared inwardly for long ages in spiritual spheres became our physical exterior—our senses, for example. Thus, as we have seen, the world that has our attention while we are awake only appears material; a spiritual world is hiding behind sensory phenomena. All that is within us, such as our organs, was formed much later; viewed cosmically it is much newer. This is why the material processes we encounter there are hidden behind the spiritual phenomena of our soul life, as we saw in chapter 1.

After death we will experience the following, as Rudolf Steiner describes:

> While on the Earth we say that in us is a lung; in us is a heart; outside us is a Sun; outside us is a Moon; outside us is a zodiac. But during the life between death and a new birth we say that in us is a zodiac; in us is the Sun; in us is the Moon; outside us is a lung; outside us is a heart. Between death and a new birth everything we now carry within our skin becomes increasingly our outer world, our universe, our cosmos. Our view of the relationship

> between world and humankind is exactly opposite when we are living between death and a new birth.*

To demonstrate being "turned," Steiner frequently took a glove and turned it inside out. Similarly, in the transition to a different kind of existence, the inside becomes the outside, and the outside the inside.

After we have died, we begin our journey, turned inside out, back through the life just ended. Our etheric body frees itself and is integrated into the etheric world. We begin to process our life experience and purify it. All we go through in the way of inner experiences on our way through the soul world and the spirit world was sketched in chapters 2 and 3. For this journey of the soul to the realms beyond time and space I have used Rudolf Steiner's description in his book *Theosophy.* At the end of chapter 2 we saw how Rudolf Steiner gave these experiences cosmic significance in lectures in 1912 and 1913;** that this inner journey turns out to be also a way through the spheres of the planets into the cosmos.

The Elemental World

Rudolf Steiner elaborated on these soul experiences in 1913 in *The Threshold of the Spiritual World*, in which he also introduced the concept of the elemental world.*** He explained that, with this kind of nomenclature, we have to bear in mind that the soul's experiences after death are completely different from those during life. This is connected with the soul's capacity to transform itself and the way it perceives sympathies and antipathies. In his book *Theosophy,* Steiner said that he chose

* Rudolf Steiner, *The Mystery of the Trinity*, p. 99.

** Rudolf Steiner, *Between Death and Rebirth.*

*** Rudolf Steiner, *A Way of Self-knowledge: And the Threshold of the Spiritual World*, p. 133.

his words as carefully as possible to characterize in the right way the soul's experiences after death.

The Threshold of the Spiritual World gives us a description of how, soon after the physical body has separated itself from the soul, the etheric body also separates. The soul then lives on for a while in the astral body. The etheric body, now independent of the soul, transforms itself within the elemental world and is absorbed into the beings who form this elemental world. The soul does not participate in this, but it does experience what occurs there after death as its *outer world.* This experience of the elemental world *from the outside* is described in the book as the soul's journey through the soul world. Depending on the point of view, this world is called "soul world" or "elemental world."

While the soul thus lives in the astral body and experiences the elemental world as its outer world, it is strongly interested in what the etheric body is experiencing. Transformations of the etheric body in that realm are, for the soul, its own outer world during the entire time it remains in kamaloka. We see how our etheric body is accepted or rejected by the beings of the elemental world, depending on our good or objectionable qualities. Going through kamaloka means, therefore, that by beholding the ever-changing experiences of the etheric body we become aware of who we must become. Our outer environment in the elemental world is formed, on the one hand, by the metamorphoses of beings who are of the same nature as our etheric body and, on the other hand, by our etheric body itself. All of this depends on the "mood" of our soul and on the way etheric substance dissolves in the elemental world. The interest of the soul in all those processes is described (as mentioned) as the soul's journey through the soul world.

Thus, being "turned inside out" happens with the transition from the physical to a suprasensory world, which we know as the etheric world. The term *elemental world* indicates that the souls of the spirits of the four elements (earth, water, air, and fire) have their home here. They have their tasks in the Earth's etheric body. Speaking of an "elemental world" could suggest that these are the only beings we perceive in that realm. In addition to the four beings of the classical elements, those of light also belong in this world. And we also find beings there whose home is in a higher spiritual realm and whose activity exceeds that of the sphere of the Earth.

Our etheric body has its corresponding aspect in this "cosmic–elemental world," a counterpart that maintains our connection with this world. During the first few days after death, when we are ourselves such an elemental being in that world, an interaction takes place between our etheric body and its counterposition that attracts the etheric body, so to speak. This was described in the introduction as the other side of letting go of the etheric body. Because the etheric body is integrated into the etheric world, we enter a relationship with the elemental beings who accompanied us from our birth until death. We could say that they group themselves in a kind of planetary system around the Sun of our etheric counterpart.

Thus the fruits of our life are gradually absorbed into the world of spirit, and all we have won and acquired during life merges into it. The soul's connection with the integrated etheric body remains in existence and can be used by the deceased to connect with the living. The etheric counterposition, said Steiner, serves in this process as a "change-over switch."*

* Rudolf Steiner, *The Connection between the Living and the Dead*, p. 146.

We can observe this second world, which is suprasensory, if we possess the suprasensory capacity of Imagination. It is also the imaginative world for which Rudolf Steiner has used the expression "astral level."

Toward Cosmic Midnight

When the soul, too, separates from the astral body, it lives on in the "I," the true "I." This does not involve turning inside out, since it is a transition between two nonphysical worlds.

After that separation, the astral body goes through a period of oblivion in a world where nothing can be experienced by means of the senses or by the soul forces such as thinking, feeling, and willing, with which we are familiar in earthly life. Subsequently, as the soul continues to exist in the true "I" it experiences this world *as its outer environment*. This was described earlier as the journey of the soul through the world of the spirit. The meaning of this is that the soul, which experiences itself in the true "I," is surrounded by what it lived through inwardly and experienced through thinking, feeling, and the will during life. The true "I" actually lives in a world that extends beyond and above the world of spirit.

We cannot use the analogy of a snake shedding its skin to imagine what happens when the astral body begins to separate itself from the true "I," in which we then live on. We do not, so to say, slither out of our astral body, which then stays behind somewhere. Rather, the astral body loosens itself everywhere from us; it grows larger and larger until it has merged into the entire environment surrounding us. In other words, we experience ourselves as standing at the center of our spiritual environment. We see how the astral body grows larger in all directions so that we now see our spiritual environment permeated by our astral body, which becomes ever more indistinct in the process. We still feel we are within the astral body, but we also feel freed of it.

To characterize this astonishing feeling, Steiner used the image of a swarm of gnats. When it is at some distance away we see the swarm move as a black mass; when the gnats disperse, we no longer see a swarm.* What we experience with the astral body is similar to this. In the end we lose it, and thus our connection with everything we lived through on Earth also breaks completely away. We see our inner being disappear into the spiritual world. Now, altruistic, selfless souls will keep the connection with the life they lived for a long time; egoistic souls are quickly submerged into the state of oblivion caused by the disappearance of the astral body. In *Theosophy,* Steiner described this experience of the astral body being absorbed and dispersed as the actual spirit realm.

Once everything we can remember has disappeared, it returns in another way; then it also shows how our next life will have to manifest according to the nature of our past lives. Our future destiny then comes to meet us from distant cosmic spaces, concentrating itself in our center. Thus we go through a period of complete oblivion at approximately the middle of our journey between death and the next birth, and we experience ourselves purely in our true "I."

We can go through this time of oblivion in a kind of spiritual sleep of the soul. However, if we have prepared ourselves sufficiently, we can experience the transition from the memory of prior lives to a vision of destiny in succeeding lives as a kind of *"cosmic midnight hour."*

* Rudolf Steiner, *Secrets of the Threshold*, p. 140.

Metamorphosis of Soul Powers

Not only are we completely turned inside out in this way and our whole orientation changed, but also the forces of our soul go through a metamorphosis. For example, faith, hope, and love help to unlock spiritual domains for the soul after death (as we saw in chapter 2) once the soul begins to find its way in its own world.

When the tableau of our life fades after the etheric body separates, soul capacities are freed that were integral parts of the body during earthly life. The first of these are the forces underlying memory. Our memory, which we could say was transformed toward the spirit, begins to become a power of perception. Then we make an unsettling discovery; we see that we are surrounded by beings of our own creation, and we recognize in them what we thought during life on Earth. Now that we are trying to "keep our eyes open" in the elemental spiritual world, we see how beings reveal themselves—beings that during life seemed to be mere thoughts. All our thoughts stand fully alive around us, amid an abundance of elemental beings. They themselves tell us how long ago we created them. They surrounded us even during earthly life as our "own" elemental beings; now we become aware of them, and we become acquainted with the elemental world through them. Moreover, we eventually also get to know and, more important, learn to distinguish the elemental beings that live in this world independently of us.

This is what happens to our thoughts and memories. Things are different for our feelings and will, of which we were never quite aware during life. In feelings and the will, our connection with the past life continues for years. Even for those who die in old age, there were nevertheless things they longed for and wanted to do. After death, we eventually need to cut all ties to longings and desires; we have to overcome the attractions exerted on us by life in a physical body. During the time this takes in kamaloka, we need a detour through the past life for all that we experienced there. In this way we can, for example, come into contact with those to whom we were close and loved. Becoming familiar with our own elemental beings, we learn to discern in those of others what their thoughts are and what lives in their souls as memory and in relation to the feeling realm of our own past life.

Thus, in this phase we connect with what belongs to us only through what was our feeling and will in earthly life. We are able to "feel" as we felt during life; living in those feelings, we come into contact with those with whom we are connected. However, we cannot progress in this unless feeling and will die and are transformed—unless they become "feeling–longing" or "longing–feeling." We could also say "willing permeated by feeling" and "feeling permeated by willing."* We must gradually develop a will that flows out of ourselves toward living thought beings, permeating them with a feeling that swims on the waves of this will. When the will then encounters such an elemental being and is thrown back, it does not return as will but as a wave of feeling returning to us. Thus our own being lives, poured out into the cosmos as feeling that returns to us on the waves of the will. The beings in the elemental world begin to become real to us, and we gradually perceive what is present around us as the outer spiritual world.

Creative Soul Power

As our time in kamaloka progresses, our life on Earth falls away from us, and we can develop a soul force that no longer

* Rudolf Steiner, *The Inner Nature of Man*, p. 69.

resembles what we found familiar on Earth. We begin to experience how the soul becomes immensely active and radiates activity into its surroundings. The environment becomes visible to the soul because it shines light on it through its creative soul force. The soul, we might say, becomes its own sun.

We thus expand on the ocean of our will with feeling–longing, waves of feeling that come back to us and with which we perceive the living, floating, and objective thought beings in the world of spirit. We also begin to feel at home in our new environment because of the soul light that gradually awakes in us as a creative spiritual light force. During life, that force was hidden deeply within us as the force that maintained life and consciousness. In the world of spirit, it enables us to adapt amid the realities in which we tentatively move, appearing to us in the light that shines from our own soul.

Here we notice that we have a personal horizon. The spiritual world opens to us to the extent that we have acquired such capacities during life. One soul creates a wider horizon for itself than another does. This is how the soul lives its life during the first half of its journey between death and a subsequent birth.

Now we begin to notice that we cannot always remain in the condition that the soul lets its spiritual light force shine out into its surroundings, enabling us to perceive human souls, other beings, and spiritual processes. The soul feels its spiritual light force diminishing and becoming dull. It can no longer go outside but has to concentrate on itself. Thus the soul experiences alternating conditions; it pours itself out into its environment, followed by a life of inner loneliness. With regularity similar to that with which waking and sleeping alternate during life on Earth, spiritual loneliness now alternates with a spiritually sociable life; spiritual togetherness with all those other beings alternates with spiritual loneliness. During the time that the soul leads a spiritual life completely alone, it cannot look back at its times of spiritually sociable life; it has to become inwardly active and creative during that time. Alone in ourselves, we create a world that teems and moves outside and around us.

In this way, our lonely life becomes increasingly rich and extended; it experiences a strengthened consciousness and an ever-increasing light force. This gives us the strength to open again to the outside, to awake spiritually and experience spiritual companionship until the light force of the soul begins to dim, and we increasingly experience a whole world, or cosmos, in ourselves. We become more and more alone and less and less aware of what lives around us; we can now have only inner experiences. We experience infinite worlds that fill our inner being spiritually and no longer have contact with beings outside our own soul.

A New Soul Light

We have reached the midpoint of existence between death and a new birth, the "midnight" point, when we live so completely within ourselves that we are left with only a vague awareness of the beings in the spiritual world beyond our own soul. We know only that beyond the limits of our soul there are a spiritual world and spiritual beings. In a kind of spiritual darkness and absorbed in our self we experience a "cosmic midnight."* Once the soul's light force can no longer shine even into our own inner world, this self-experience becomes unbearable, and we get the feeling that we will also lose this world. However, the soul does not reach the point of losing this world, too.

* Ibid., p. 92.

In the total isolation of our cosmic midnight, a strong longing begins to arise in us. It is not the kind of longing we experienced on Earth, which we know cannot be satisfied in any way, but an extremely active longing that connects us to the world from which we have been torn. We experience this longing as a spiritual reality, a creative, formative force, and even as a new power of perception. It becomes a new kind of soul light that evokes a world that is both outer and inner; it is the world of our previous incarnations. Previous lives are recalled to our spiritual eye, and an urge arises in us to compensate in a new life for what we experienced in prior lives and to complete what remained unfinished. We want to retrieve the thoughts we observed outside ourselves—our own thought beings as well as those of many other people. However, we find that we cannot do this unless we call them back into our subsequent life.

Those other people will include, for example, those with whom we have incurred all sorts of guilt or obligations and people who are guilty or obligated in connection with us. Now we feel the need to compensate for "debts" incurred. The same urge rises in those others, and spiritual forces are awakened that strive toward Earth. The first to come into view are those with whom we were closely connected, including family members. Then there are those who shared our religious faith, for instance, and those who belonged to the same ethnic or national identity. Finally, there are the people with whom we shared ideals and spiritual life. According to the way they appear in our field of vision, we become aware of how our new life will have to be and how it proceeds from the past life.

This is the beginning of our web of destiny. We create the fundamental picture of our next life on Earth from these impressions, which are growing stronger. It becomes the "I" that will connect at our conception with what the two new parents provide.

The Heavenly Hierarchies

Now that we know the soul and spirit in their outer spiritual worlds, we need to consider the angels, who bring about the connection with our spiritual world outside, as it were. Generally, when we use the word *angels,* we include a whole world of spiritual beings and an array of angelic realms in which developments also occur. Today it must be true that there are angels who more than ever want to penetrate the purely spiritual, while others feel connected with the other, centripetal spiritual world—angels who, we might say, look up and angels who look down, and thus connect with the worlds above or the worlds below them.

We speak of nine hierarchies of angels, but we really mean the nine "choirs of angels," realms of angels that appear in three main groups, or "hierarchies." The activities of one of these hierarchies are dedicated to the Father, another to the Son, and another to the Holy Spirit. We have considered the angels of the nine angelic realms in each of the previous chapters, except for chapter 2 on the soul world. This is not surprising since that chapter describes the experiences of the soul in its outer world after death; the angels are part of this world only to the extent that they also play a role in life on Earth. We also saw that angels cannot immediately be with the deceased, for as long as they do not yet have anything in common.

The spiritual beings of the third hierarchy are the Angels, Archangels, and Archai. From the lowest choir of this hierarchy, the ninth angelic realm, the Angels brought the message of the Resurrection to humankind. We become aware of these angels after death when we have sufficiently adapted to their world;

this is in the Moon sphere, the closest to human beings. The realm of the Archangels coincides roughly with the sphere of Mercury, and that of the Archai with the Venus sphere. The spiritual beings of the second hierarchy—the Exousiai, Dynamis, and Kyriotetes—form the spiritual essence of the Sun. The Dynamis also work into the sphere of Mars, and the Kyriotetes into that of Jupiter. The Thrones, the first choir of the highest hierarchy appear in the sphere of Mars, and also work into the sphere of Saturn. The Cherubim begin to appear in the Jupiter sphere, and the Seraphim in the Saturn sphere.

As we try to familiarize ourselves with the spheres of the angels, we are dealing with a world known to ancient human beings. With Copernicus, a worldview came into being that reckoned the Sun as the center of the solar system. "Reckoned," indeed, because a system in which the heavenly bodies orbit around the Sun is something we can calculate. The more ancient view was connected with the development of humankind and the Earth, and thus experienced the Earth as its center. People at that time found the domain of the angelic realms by imagining spheres in space extending around the Earth, up to the paths of the planets. A planet in that worldview is, so to speak, a moving marker of such a sphere and denotes its limits.

The names of the angelic realms offer some indication of how they are connected with the development of human beings and the Earth. In the highest hierarchy, the Seraphim, or Spirits of Love, form the substance of our entire universe, whereas the Cherubim, or Spirits of Harmony, are those who bear the whole development in their consciousness. Our universe was able to manifest because the Thrones, or Spirits of Will, made the pure nature of their spiritual essence available. In the second hierarchy, pure spiritual light proceeds from the Spirits of

Wisdom, the Kyriotetes, and awakes the capacity to radiate life back to them in this manifesting universe. Pure warmth proceeds from the Spirits of Movement, or Dynamis, with the result that something like soul movement arises in this universe. So that individual forms can arise, the lowest angelic beings of the second hierarchy—the Spirits of Form, or Exousiai—creates individualization in manifesting life.

The highest choir of the angels of the third hierarchy—the Archai, or Spirits of Personality—bestows the character of personality on those individual forms in that origination. Through the activities of the second choir, the Archangels, or Spirits of Fire, the beginning of a kind of inner life, a "light life," arises, flaring up and then dying down again. Finally, the Angels, or Sons of Twilight, who form the ninth angelic realm (the lowest choir of the third hierarchy), bring about something like a primitive metabolism in this beginning of a universe. They are also called Sons of Life.*

After death, when we are completely absorbed into ourselves, we enter the domain of the angels of the third hierarchy. Gradually we develop an inner relationship with them. They are connected with the inner world with which we are so busy at first, bringing us into contact with our spiritual outer world during this phase. After a while, we come to know an objective spiritual world, the spiritual world outside us. The angels of the second hierarchy lead us on this path; with them and with the third hierarchy we then begin to work on our coming destiny. The angels of the first hierarchy help us so that this future destiny can become reality.

* These names were introduced by Rudolf Steiner in *An Outline of Esoteric Science*, chapter 6, "Cosmic and Human Evolution Now and in the Future."

7

Reversal: Downside Turns Up

What is the human being? We asked this question before. What is this mortal being who nonetheless has a future? This question accompanies us all the way to a new birth, asked in an increasingly personal way. Along the way we receive an equally personal answer. We will know what we are as a human being—who we were, what we have become, and how we can become in the future. We receive our own answer according to our penetration of the first future homeland, the realm of spirit.

What is the human being, really? It is a question Rudolf Steiner repeatedly asked in a lecture on April 6, 1919.* A week earlier he had, as a prelude, reminded the same audience that we have to consider the whole world before we can find an answer to this question. The small world of a human being, the microcosm, is not understandable unless we recognize how it comes into being from the greater world. And we have to be especially realistic in our view of the connections between the world in which we live between birth and death and the one in which we exist from death until a new birth.

For instance, what do those who have died perceive of our language, the Earth as such, and the human beings who live there? The observation of how the soul finds its expression in what we might call a certain form is a bridge for us to reach mutual understanding. As we saw in chapter 4, Steiner could

* Rudolf Steiner, *Vergangenheits- und Zukunftsimpulse im sozialen Geschehen* (Impulses of the past and future in social events), Apr. 6, 1919.

describe the transformation of the deceased in the worlds of soul and spirit with the aid of physiognomy. Through such mutual observations, beings who live only as soul–spirit entities and embodied beings on the Earth develop mutual understanding in a concrete sense.

To answer the question of what a human being is, in his lecture of April 6, 1919, Steiner used a few recent historical examples to show how we need thoughts that include the suprasensory aspect. We have pretty much lost the capacity to think "inclusively," keeping the spiritual components of an outer and inner development in view. For instance, who still considers the three aspects of our development during life with a spiritually trained mind?

First, we have our talents, natural aptitudes, and gifts. These are not understandable unless we know that they arise through the interplay between the suprasensory before birth and the heredity we receive at conception. In our interaction with other people during life, we subsequently develop all kinds of proficiencies, such as language and personal ways of conducting ourselves as social beings. We also gain life experience by learning what to do or refrain from doing in all kinds of situations, as well as by developing a sense of what lives behind the scenes, what rises from the depths. However, we cannot answer the question of what is the human being concretely for ourselves except through life experience as we learn how to deal with the crises presented by life.

For example, we might notice that around the age of twenty-seven or twenty-eight we no longer grow inwardly as a matter of course but instead reach a kind of boundary where we have to handle our development consciously. Then there is the midlife crisis, whereby we discover that we are not progressing in our career, or we have become a stranger in our marriage and family. Do we have the capacity to maintain continuity consciously with ourselves through some effort, or do we need to look for new connections elsewhere, which in the end might simply repeat the old ones and fall away just as easily? Do not look for examples in fantastic superheroes. Don't let yourself be seduced by intimate, psychologizing navel-gazing. Dare to face your situation concretely and, in the process, don't forget the suprasensory component. Then the question of our humanness can become concrete.

Anthroposophy can be an exceptional help to us as human beings because it takes us out of our self-centeredness, our inclination to put our self at the center of everything and to view matters from our own point of view. For example, I have just indicated that outer influences have meaning for our inner development only until around age twenty-eight. Isn't it therefore necessary, having read something like this, to begin self-observation, with painful precision, throughout that phase of life? Should at a later age worry about how this was for us back then? It is especially such subjective essentials that we should try to approach objectively without applying them to ourselves; we should learn to view them as spiritual facts in the whole of human evolution.

The foregoing description of our threefold inner life hints at a view of the human being that Rudolf Steiner started speaking of publicly in 1917.

The Threefold Human Being

The threefold nature of the human organism is a truly new element in Anthroposophy. It is the culmination of all the work that Steiner accomplished beginning in 1882, the year he was asked to edit Goethe's natural scientific writings for publication. In concise terms, he described this view of the human being in the sixth addendum to *Riddles of the Soul,* published in 1917. In the following year, he elaborated on this concept, especially in connection with its pedagogical and social consequences. This view of being human finds its social equivalent in what is called the threefold social organism.

We encounter the threefold nature of our organism every day. We know one another as acting human beings through our own will. We become aware of feelings, emotions, and conscience in ourselves and in others. We all stand in the world as thinking, observing humans with personal mental pictures and ideas. These three soul functions are connected with three areas we find in ourselves as the three systems in our organism.

First is the upper pole, our brain and the senses, or nerve–sense system. Then we have the organs of rhythm, our heart and lungs, in the central, the rhythmic area. And in the lower pole we find the organs of metabolism and movement, including the liver, intestines, and muscles. This is why we can call the lower pole the metabolic and limb system. The upper pole is the home of our thinking and mental picturing; feeling belongs to the middle; and willing to the lower pole.

When we contemplate these three regions, we become aware that we can distinguish them but not separate them. They interpenetrate in the body; for instance, we can observe with all parts of the body. Feeling and the will express themselves throughout the body, but the three soul functions each have a special relationship to a specific area. Our life of imagination and mental pictures has a physical counterpart in the nervous system, our feeling life in the rhythm of breathing and blood circulation, and the will in the metabolism. Since these systems overlap, as it were, and do not exist separately and side-by-side, our soul functions are present throughout the body; the will thus has its bodily counterpart in every area where metabolic processes take place, not just in the actual metabolism in the lower body.

Although the upper pole is therefore more than just the head, the head in particular represents the nerve–sense system, just as the chest represents the rhythmic system, while the lower body and limbs represent the lower pole. We can see a reflection, or revelation, of the cosmos in human beings, who appear in this way as a threefold entity on Earth. We see this same threefold nature in the cosmic primeval form of the human being.

First let's consider the head, which is the "deadest" part of the body and whose spherical shape recalls its cosmic origin. Viewed cosmically, the head is essentially the result of our life in the previous incarnation. More or less due to the forces of heredity, the body grows onto it each time. This body will become the head in the next incarnation in a metamorphosed form. Most of the work in the world of spirit involves the formation of the head.

In the organs of the chest, especially the heart and lungs, we find the second reflection of the cosmos, not in the form of a sphere, but a half sphere, forces that come from the east as a half circle. We find the third reflection in the organs of the lower body and limbs. They are formed primarily during the mother's pregnancy under the influence of forces that come from the center of the Earth, differentiated according to the area where the parents and ancestors live. This threefold human being is formed and differentiated as a whole by the forces of the Earth's entire environment.

We recognize here the human being who (as described in chapter 1) goes the first part of the way from death to a new birth in four phases toward the Sun.

In this human entity, the members have their own place during life. The "I," for example, is related to the lower body, where everything still happens unconsciously, as in deep sleep. Like the metabolism, our true "I" is unconscious in us; it cannot become active until our ordinary "I" has left the body during sleep. The astral body finds its instruments in the chest area, and the heart beats because of its influence. The etheric body is bound to the head, where the reflection of our "I" becomes conscious to us—the concept, the mental picture of it in the everyday "I."

The Human Being on Earth

When we observe the human being on the Earth we can notice that of the three areas of our constitution only the middle one, the rhythmic system of heartbeat and respiration, has gone through regular development. The head is clearly past its prime. In evolution, when we place the human being after the animals at the end of a long path of physical development we discover that our head has not really developed further physically. It has actually regressed in its development; it has undergone involution. Rudolf Steiner pointed out, for instance, that we are not absorbed in our observations; we become emotionally involved in them only when we process them, not while the observation takes place. Since the soul is not bound so much by bodily processes, the human being has developed space for the evolution of soul and spirit. This makes it possible for both our previous incarnation and our life between death and rebirth to influence our organism.

This is reversed in the lower pole, the limb area, where development has gone too far. This is why the limb system serves us not only in this life, but also in the life that begins at death. In its spiritual–psychic form, we clearly carry our future (which begins at death) with us in our limb system.*

However, in the way we live as human beings on Earth in our time—we should be fully aware of this—we are more a twofold than a threefold being. Our inner being is actually fully alive only in our metabolic area and the lower part of our rhythmic system, where we can have an inner life. In the upper part of our rhythmic area and in our nerve–sense system, we are oriented to what has become a completely outer world. We perceive this outer world with our senses; we process our impressions with our intellect. We breathe the outer air, which fills the lungs.

In all these actions, we are not much more than a processing station. All of nature is present in what flows into our upper pole: colors, stars, sounds, clouds, and the air itself. But this mass of impressions is reduced today into a limited, sensory outer world. We don't find much there that is related to our inner world—no elemental beings or gods, as ancient peoples were able to experience. We no longer find spirit there. It might be that even the last little remnant of inner life in our extensive lower pole is actually not much more than a reflection of processes in the metabolic system. When we have problems with our intestines or in one of our organs, we may experience this in the soul as a huge inner problem at which we can stare ourselves blind.

In our threefold nature, we are pictures of the suprasensory and differentiated forces at work there. The forces that form the head go back to the soul as it was before conception, and the most important elements in the formation of the head arise from our behavior, our actions, indeed even in part from feelings during our previous incarnation. The lower pole of the

* Rudolf Steiner, *Dying Earth and Living Cosmos,* May 14, 1918.

body is formed much less individually; everything is still open to what will arise in this life. The middle is formed by the interplay of forces from the environment in which the soul sojourns in the spiritual world between our lives on Earth. What surrounded the soul between its previous death and new conception and birth is interwoven with what will surround it between the coming death and subsequent conception and birth. A living image of this is the process of breathing out and breathing in.

We could view ourselves as perennial plants, except that our "root system" is always rejuvenated. We can actually view the human being as an inverted plant. The plant reaches for the sun with its leaves and blossoms, but it roots are in the earth. As human beings, we have our roots in the world of spirit and return to Earth with our organs. We can do this because our root system, which is partially formed by our behavior, actions, and feelings, forms new roots in the spirit after each life.

Sun Existence

Having considered the threefold nature of the human being, we can turn to our spiritual Sun existence. We need the image of the threefold human being to understand all that takes place in the spiritual Sun existence. So now we can pick up that thread from the end of chapter 5, which was interrupted.

We experienced the first big change—our being turned inside out—as we entered the suprasensory world, through which we could begin to adapt to a nonphysical world. In Sun existence, we begin to prepare for our next life by recasting our whole spiritual appearance. In this development, below becomes above, and we will not leave this sphere until we have begun our descent toward our next life. Work takes place on the spiritual form of our future head in the Sun sphere, and this continues into the Saturn sphere and in the outer universe after that. Spiritual Sun existence extends far beyond the actual Sun sphere itself.

In the spiritual Sun sphere, we live between death and rebirth in the heart of the world, and we spend more time there than anywhere else. We came to know it as the region of soul life, the highest region of the soul world and the domain of the second spiritual hierarchy. The forces working here are primarily those of the feeling life. Moreover, what Rudolf Steiner called our "suprasensory circle of acquaintances" grows ever larger here.*

The recasting that will lift the below to the above—remaking the lower pole of our body into the upper pole—begins with the gradual transformation of the legs into the spiritual form of the lower jaw, and the arms into the upper jaw and cheekbones. In the subsequent planetary spheres this beginning of a head is imprinted with several skills, which will be described further on. All that will belong to the archetype of the human head is then formed in the realm beyond Saturn, the realm of the fixed stars. The archetypes of the inner organs are formed on the way through the planetary spheres to the realms beyond them, as well as on the way back to the Sun sphere.

In Sun existence, "the world beyond" enters our consciousness—the Earth as such. Something happens next that we all know in some way or other if we have ever immersed ourselves in history; we encounter an event or situation that we recognize. We get the feeling: *This is strange—as if I were there!* Those who only recently encountered the concept of reincarnation

* Rudolf Steiner, *At Home in the Universe*, p. 64.

may then be inclined to think that maybe they were actually there in their latest incarnation on Earth. But this isn't necessarily true, because we might have received such strong impressions precisely in the year when we had our most vivid connection with the Earth and witnessed those things at that time from the spiritual world. In describing this, Steiner indicated a period from 370 to 420 years in the past.*

Knowing that this experience occurs might be important today, because during the last decades of the twentieth century there were reports of people who were deeply convinced that they returned soon after their death in the concentration camps of World War II. It is striking how easily people seized on the idea of reincarnation to explain memories that weighed on them. However, should we really recognize objective remnants of a prior life in such reincarnation images? What is going on here? (See appendix 4.)

Future Destiny

Souls that belong together are carried into the spiritual Sun sphere by the forces of the inner planets. They arrive there with everything they went through together, but also bring with them the seeds of their shared future destiny. This totality of human souls shines into the cosmos, along with the judgments that the angels of the second and third hierarchies have passed on their "heavenly worth." In the meantime, we have adopted the form of the Sun in our spiritual appearance. Our whole physiognomy has become round, and when we arrive in the Sun sphere we become a spiritual globe, so to speak, in which the universe is reflected. We become one complete spiritual

* Ibid. p. 65.

sense organ, and we feel united with our whole experience of ourselves and others. Next, the time comes when we will feel connected with the angels of the first heavenly hierarchy.

So long as we moved in our moral, spiritual physiognomy among people with whom we knew were connected with us by destiny, we sojourned in the domain of the third hierarchy, the Angels, Archangels, and Archai. After that, planetary forces took us into spiritual Sun existence, where we also connected with the second hierarchy, the Exousiai, Dynamis, and Kyriotetes. When we sense that we have become part of the whole universe in our own Sun existence, we also connect with the first hierarchy, the Thrones, Cherubim, and Seraphim. At this point, we can generate interest in those with whom we were not yet connected by destiny, those who came close to us during the life just ended. In our new life, we will also be connected through destiny with them.

We now become aware of an important metamorphosis that takes place in those with whom we were more or less closely connected by destiny under the influence of the Seraphim, Cherubim, and Thrones. Our destiny begins to take form in a movement like that of the limbs; the way we lived our destiny begins to be expressed in something like the circulation of blood. Here, in the midnight hour of our existence between death and a new birth, all those who are connected with one another now work on each other, depending on the closeness of their connection. We observe how organs are transformed in a metamorphosis of the entire lower pole of the human being into the upper pole. We don't do this by ourselves and not just for ourselves; we work on one another. Thus spiritual ties are formed that cause us to find each other in life, so that we will come together with those people. It is particularly the spiritual form of the new head that is fashioned in this destiny connection of people who belong together.

Everything that is thus transformed in the middle of our life between death and rebirth has a moral–spiritual quality. When the upper pole of the human-being-of-the-past-life has gradually faded away, the lower pole of that human-being-of-the-past-life is spiritually transformed into the upper pole of the human-being-of-the-next-life. What is thus transformed now begins to sound; it becomes cosmic music. Having become an image of the Sun itself, a mirror of the universe, the external human figure is heard as sound. Eventually, what was initially only a harmony of sounds will adopt the forms of the spiritual cosmic word. Human beings then speak their own being from the universe, and divine–spiritual beings in the universe can observe them.

When we want to describe human beings at the beginning of their journey through the planetary spheres, we have to be aware of their initial spiritual form. However, such a form gradually disappears in the spheres of the inner planets, and in Sun existence we adopt the spiritual form of the Sun. Living in Sun existence, we immerse ourselves in the sounds of cosmic music. In cosmic harmonies, we perceive the meaning of collaboration among the spiritual beings who find their expression in the stars. Here, our feeling life is powerfully addressed; we feel how those harmonies vibrate melodiously within us. We contribute to these sounds ourselves, albeit with dissonant tones, since we are still dragging along a remnant of our earthly existence, the final remnants of our capacity of speech. Through the dissonant tones we produce in Sun existence, the spiritual beings learn what they need to do to counter the progressive degeneration on Earth.

Therefore, there is first the contact of those who are connected with one another in their spiritual physiognomy and are thus able to perceive each other—contact based on an inner vision that brings people together. Next is mutual understanding, knowing that there will be a joint future because of shared destiny in the past. Finally, based on deep insight, we mutually work on one another, and what is fashioned spiritually in this way transforms itself into sound and speech. We then speak a warm, creative word to each other. Thus a being that has become word meets a being that has become word; a permeable soul meets another permeable soul. We merge into one another. When people on Earth meet and feel sympathy or antipathy toward each other, this feeling reflects what they went through with and in each other in the middle period between death and a new birth, the time when we were able to become completely united with each other.

Once we have completed this time, we gradually leave the domain of the first heavenly hierarchy and return to that of the second hierarchy, where the forces of the planets work on each other. We no longer live enclosed by the bonds of shared destiny; we begin to perceive a world outside ourselves. We come to know relationships among beings with whom we have had none and to discover relationships with human souls who have just emerged for us in the middle of the time between death and the next birth.

Spiritual beginnings, especially those of the malleable forms of the new chest and new limbs, are formed increasingly into the spiritual archetype of the coming human figure. What in us had become cosmic word becomes the music of the spheres again, and the music of the spheres becomes the newly formed human being. Then the time approaches when we can connect with the embryonic seed of the human being on Earth, given to us by our father and mother; the spiritual form of the human being can now embody itself anew.

Four Worlds

All of this takes place in four worlds that we may call ours. Rudolf Steiner described these in *At Home in the Universe,* a lecture cycle given in The Hague during November 1923. On our journey from life to death and to a new life we come to know these four worlds.

The *first world* is the physical world, the world that we know through our senses, where everything is perceptible and is physical in nature.

Bordering on our physical, perceptible world is a *second world,* which is not immediately perceptible to sensory observation. It is suprasensory and penetrates our physical world, where its effects can be observed. Our etheric body is part of this world; the world in which the third heavenly hierarchy, the Angels, Archangels, and Archai, live. Also here are the human beings who are with the third hierarchy between death and a new birth.

The *third world* is also suprasensory, just as the etheric world is, but what is remarkable here is that it is actually perceptible from our physical world; it reaches into our world but is usually not well recognized as such. Part of this suprasensory world, for instance, is everything that streams into us in the light from the Sun. The spiritual beings dwelling on the Sun are suprasensory, but they are also perceptible on Earth. However, we do not usually interpret the form in which they appear correctly; the same is true of the beings who send their light to us from the stars. The second heavenly hierarchy, the

Exousiai, Dynamis, and Kyriotetes, dwell in this suprasensory though perceptible world.

The *fourth world* again is not perceptible but, as is the first world, it is physical—physical, but not perceptible, such as gravity, which can be experienced but not perceived. What was at one time called the mercurial and appears in the form of the drops with which we are familiar as mercury also cannot be perceived; this is similar to what is present in us as protein, for instance. The first hierarchy, the Thrones, Cherubim, and Seraphim, live in this invisible–physical world.

Each time we die and leave our world, we are pulled into the invisible, suprasensory etheric, elemental world, where the third hierarchy lives. We have disappeared from our world, as it were, into this invisibility. Next we enter the perceptible–suprasensory world of the second hierarchy, where we come to understand our destiny in the streaming light of the Sun and the stars, where we see how the web of destiny manifests. Deceased, ostensibly dead human beings are present here.

Reversing direction, we then make the metamorphosis toward the Earth to prepare ourselves for our next perceptible physical life. We already live on Earth again, except that in this period between death and a new birth we are moving in the invisible physical.

With death, we are "turned" from life to the invisible; we re-enter life invisibly, "turned" again, to immerse ourselves in our future life in the perceptible, physical world.

In the midnight hour of our existence in the world of spirit, we find ourselves in invisible physical life, in which we not only move among people who live physically on Earth, but also move among those who are going through the midnight hour of their own existence.

Mineral, Physical, and Material

I have spoken about "physical" worlds and "supraphysical" worlds. What is meant by *physical?* We call the body in which we live on Earth a physical body. But that might be misleading, because "physical" as a concept comes across as something solid. This is because our earthly body is a physical–mineral body, one that obeys physical laws and is filled with mineral substances. *Physical* therefore tells us that there are laws that might appear in a variety of conditions, such as in solid matter, in water and air, and in the various kinds of ethers. The physical could even appear as etheric or astral. This is why we have to distinguish between outer appearances and inner laws.

At the current stage of development of our Earth, "physical" coincides with "material." We can *see* a physical body; we can *touch* it because sensory matter, the matter of the visible physical world, is lodged in the suprasensory system of physical forces, which have formed a body as an expression of physical laws. What we know as "mineral" is a suprasensory form body, a structure of forces of a certain cosmic age that appears as physical, mineral materiality. On Earth we have the mineral realm in its material form.

On Earth, matter is also spirit, but it is "broken spirit." In 1911 Steiner said, "Matter is a heap of ruins of the spirit."*

Whenever something has received form, but also wherever still-formless thought beings exist as seeds, we know that spiritual beings are at work. Chapter 3 gave an impression of this with the description of the fifth, sixth, and seventh regions of spirit land. Therefore, what is called "supraphysical" in the

* Rudolf Steiner, *The World of the Senses and the World of the Spirit*, p. 52.

picture of the four worlds is an expression of different kinds of suprasensory laws from those with which we are familiar in our physical world.

Do we really need such an elaboration of physical and supraphysical worlds and all these remarks on mineral, physical, and material? I thought they might help us to "ground" our mental pictures of life after death and the formation of destiny that take place there. We have to be able to give the images evoked by Rudolf Steiner's descriptions a place in our own world. We learn to view our world with different eyes when we hear that the deceased, at the zenith of their existence, are right here in the midst of us. The first future homeland for all of us in the realm of the spirit is, suprasensorially and supraphysically, invisibly present in our here and now.

Such concrete pictures will be useful when the thread is taken up again in the story of our future destiny.

8

A Revised and Improved Edition

In Philadelphia, the tombstone on the grave of the American statesman and scholar Benjamin Franklin, at his wish, mentions only his name and the year of his death. As a young man of twenty-two, at the beginning of a full life, he drew up the following epitaph for himself:

> The Body of B. Franklin, printer,
> Like the Cover of an old Book,
> Its Contents torn out,
> And stripped of its Lettering and Gilding,
> Lies here, Food for Worms.
> But the Work shall not be wholly lost:
> For it will, as he believed, appear once more,
> In a new & more perfect Edition,
> Corrected and Amended by the Author.

A fairly detailed picture! We begin to work in all seriousness on this new and more perfect edition when we leave the Sun sphere, after which we no longer carry with us any remnant of our earthly life. The influence of spiritual Sun existence will remain with us throughout the preparation for our next life in the planetary spheres we enter after leaving that region. However, we are truly not alone in this correction and amendment of "the work"; a great, let's say, "editorial team" assists us.

In what follows we describe this path of the spiritual human form, now viewed from a physiognomic perspective.

Joint Effort

We have adopted the spiritual form of the Sun; our spiritual appearance has become like the spherical form of the universe. In the spheres of the outer planets where we will be moving now, work on the spiritual design of our future head continues in the metamorphosis of the lower pole of the last life into the design of the lower and upper jaws and cheekbones for the coming life. In chapter 3, through the description of the various regions of spirit land we came to know these spheres as the lowest regions of the spirit realm and in chapter 6 that the experiences of the soul continue to exist in the true human "I," whereas the astral body is gradually absorbed into a world where we are no longer reminded of anything on Earth.

First we enter the sphere of Mars and, in particular, experience its population, part of which is formed by human souls. Having left the immediate realm of the Sun, these are, insofar as we are concerned, the souls of only those who, like ourselves, died an earthly death. Beings of the higher hierarchies who form this sphere enable the creative word to resound in the universe from their whole being. In the Mars realm, cosmic music becomes cosmic language; music that fills the universe here sounds like a language that is not imitative or descriptive but creative. We are gradually woven into it once we have learned to listen to it. Here we are students of the masters of the creative word.

In the realm we enter next, that of Jupiter, we encounter the spiritual beings who watch over cosmic thoughts. They creatively radiate beings who are pure thought into our planetary system and its environment. This is why we can experience another transformation on our way through the Jupiter realm. As a mirror image of the spherical form of the universe, leaving the remainders of earthly language behind, we have learned to let cosmic music resound creatively in us without producing dissonance ourselves.

On our journey through the Mars and Jupiter realms, we come to know the creative language, the creative thoughts of the universe. Into the spiritual germ of our future head is implanted the capacity to begin to understand the universe—the universe, mind you, not the Earth. On Earth we had knowledge of minerals, plants, and animals, but here in the planetary spheres we gain insight into the secrets of the spiritual universe. Through speaking, we learn the names of wondrous, lofty hierarchical beings. As we move among the beings here, called gods in some cultures, we also come to understand what they creatively bring into existence in the universe.

When we have thus learned the language and thoughts of the gods of our planetary system, then, in our sojourn in the realm of Saturn, we will come to know the total memory of those gods. In the spiritual germ of our head, everything is preformed that enables us to be a citizen of the cosmos. We then live among the beings of the heavenly hierarchies, just as we lived on Earth among minerals, plants, and animals.

Now that we can move in the macrocosm in our spiritual archetypal form, we leave the realm of the planets and are ready to enter the sphere of the fixed stars, the background for all the planetary movements—we enter the higher regions of spirit land. Here the forces from the infinite world of spirit of the Triune God can further form everything that will be part of the archetypal form of our future head.

On our way back, on the return to our future life, we pass through the planetary spheres in the reverse direction. Just as in the ascent, in the descent we experience rhythmically changing states of pouring our self out into our surroundings, alternating with concentrating within ourselves. Because we have absorbed the planetary memory in our first sojourn in Saturn existence, we can now be imprinted with the fundamentals of our personal memory capacity. What was cosmic now receives a human, earthly nuance; cosmic memory becomes the capacity of human memory.

In this second passage through the Saturn sphere, the metamorphosis of the lower pole into the upper pole is elaborated in detail. It is a tremendous work there that human beings who are interconnected by destiny accomplish in each other. They are supported in this by beings of the divine hierarchies, the Seraphim, Cherubim, and Thrones, who know how human heads have to be formed from the cosmos. Those who would ask here what the human being is, receive an answer: *This is the human being, the being on whom the highest angels perform such grand work.*

The capacity to think human thoughts arises through beholding the thoughts of the gods during the first passage through the Jupiter sphere, when later the spiritual germ of our head will have united with the growing embryo. Thereafter, in Mars existence, the spiritual germ is laid for our new bodily systems—chest and limbs—that are added to our new head, which was formed from the limbs of our prior life. The capacity we acquired on our first passage through the Mars region—the capacity to perceive the cosmic word—is now transformed into the substance in which the human "I" can later reveal itself. Here, the spiritual germs of the larynx and lungs are added.

Individual Preparation

Human beings leave the Sun region to travel through the world of stars, as described, and when they enter Sun existence for the second time they have united with the universe in which they were fully taken up and to which they surrendered. In our rhythmic expansion and concentration, we felt united there with the beings of the higher hierarchies, but now we begin to enclose ourselves again; we begin again to become individuals. We feel: *I am separating myself from that world. I seclude myself from it.* This takes place when the archetypal form of the heart is inserted into our spiritual form.

It is a special moment in our destiny when, passing anew through the Sun region, we receive the spiritual germ of our heart. Certainly, it is the spiritual, archetypal form of our future bodily heart, but most of all it is the concentrated essence of all we are as soul and spirit and all we are worth morally. We experience this concentration of our being with the lofty Sun beings who wield the creative forces of the planetary system, and thus of the Earth itself.

We now have an extraordinary feeling; we sense how the moral being that we are in the macrocosm comes to life in us as the beating of a heart, a spiritual heartbeat. The feeling that arises in us could be compared to what we feel on Earth when, in the macro blood circulation, we have the sensations of being human on Earth, whereas we have the sensations of the world outside us in our micro blood circulation and respiration. We know that, through our heartbeat, we are connected with the world and ourselves.

In the Sun existence and in the spiritual beating of our macrocosmic heart, so to speak, we sense how this beating is caused by a circulation that comes from the universe. In our cosmic heartbeat we experience ourself as a spiritual–moral soul being.

In this we also become aware of how, in words and sounds from the universe, the Exousiai, Dynamis, and Kyriotetes of the second hierarchy stream into us to express judgments of us as human beings in this universe. Now that the archetypal form of the human heart beats in the cosmos, the heartbeat of the world of which we are a part beats in it. We are to observe in this heart all that is formed by the deeds of the second heavenly hierarchy.

This second passage through Sun existence lasts for a long time. Just as we feel we are in the spiritual heart of the world, our gaze is directed downward to a series of ancestors, the last pair of which will become the parents from whom we are to be born.* In earthly terms, we connect with our ancestors several centuries before our birth. When we reach Venus and Mercury for the second time, insofar as possible we bring our destiny into harmony with that of our future family and those among whom we will appear. There we will also receive the archetypal forms of our remaining organs.

On our return to the Moon sphere, it is less important to occupy ourselves with things of the Earth than it was the first time. At that time, we had intense contact, whether good or bad, with the primeval teachers of humanity and with the ahrimanic beings who want to freeze all development at the point it has reached (chapter 4). We spend the time between conception and birth in the Moon sphere, preparing ourselves cosmically to become a human being on Earth again while our body is being prepared on Earth. This requires us to go through a great change in consciousness.

After death, our consciousness had to adapt to our new environment; with each subsequent planetary sphere we entered, our consciousness had to become more lucid and awake. On our return to Earth our consciousness is gradually toned down, but even in the Mercury sphere it is still much more lucid than

* Rudolf Steiner, *Dying Earth and Living Cosmos*, Mar. 19, 1918.

earthly consciousness can be. When we arrive in the Moon sphere again, our consciousness is dampened, as it were, so that in the still-dreaming young child it can act as a growth force. Our soul–spiritual being is able to unite itself with the embryo only because of such a dreaming consciousness. The body of the mother prepares our earthly body for ten lunar months, while the primeval teachers work together to transform cosmic consciousness into dreaming earthly consciousness in the Moon sphere. Thus we, as spiritual beings, are born on this Earth out of a cosmos that consists of spiritual beings. We have come to know these spiritual beings in the preceding pages through their work on our spiritual archetype.

Continuity with One's Self

This resulting new edition is the work of not only the angels, though it might look that way as long as we view the work from the standpoint of physiognomy—the metamorphosis of the spiritual human form in successive regions of the worlds of soul and spirit. However, we are also deeply involved in this process ourselves. During our passage through the spheres of planetary life, we go through a transformation of our soul forces. We saw the beginning of this in chapter 6, following a description of how we are turned completely inside out.

Memory capacity becomes perceptive power; we become aware of all that happens in our new spiritual environment. Our feeling and will, in their transformation into feeling-permeated will and into will-permeated feeling, acquaint us with the beings out there. Thanks to this creative soul force and to our becoming altogether active in our soul, we gradually feel at home in our new environment. However, we cannot always be oriented outwardly; we have periods of strong outward radiance when we are spiritually "social" and periods of spiritual solitariness that enable us to develop the strength to shine out again. Our solitariness increases until we can have only inner experiences. Thus we are in spiritual darkness when we experience a world midnight hour; infinite worlds pervade our inner being, whereas we know nothing of the world outside us.

This is the period when longing becomes inner creative power, a new kind of soul force that will give us an outside world again—an outside world that is really an inside world, since it is the world of our prior incarnations. We can then look back at our lives in the light born from the creative power of longing—but in our present time this no longer occurs on its own.

In all the first stages of life between death and the next birth we alternate inwardly between a solitary life and a spiritually interactive life. As though on wings of infinity, our consciousness expands over the whole spiritual world, but then when those wings are folded our consciousness falls back into solitude. Do we therefore risk becoming lost in cosmic spaces? How do we preserve continuity within ourselves in this alternating cosmic breathing in and out?

Ever since Christ appeared on Earth, we are able to maintain this cohesion in ourselves through the substance of Christ that flowed into the Earth's spiritual aura. We must not lose the connection with our self; we must always remember that on Earth we were this "I." It would be possible for us to lose our self while still feeling the connection with the spiritual world out there, outside us. Exactly because we have experienced our self as an "I" so strongly during earthly life, we have also consumed the forces that guarantee our identity after dying. Here, Christ has to come to our aid. Christ again comes to help us make the transition from the mortal to the future human being: he guides us into the experience of the cosmic midnight hour.

Based on the continuity with our self that is thus bestowed on us, we develop the capacity to look back at our previous lives and the periods we experienced between those lives. All of this becomes our outer world. In our existence in midnight solitariness, however, a force also needs to be born that enables us to grow beyond our self, and to get a grip on our self as a spiritual being in the spiritual world. Out of a longing that lives so strongly in us, a new light is created by the spirit that awakes us—this is the Holy Spirit. In this light that shines far beyond our own being, we awake anew in the universe.

Guilt

Observing the outside world that arises for us, we discover how infinitely much we have received from it, and thus how much we owe to it. We especially recognize all that we have experienced as joy in what we received and the value those things had for us—how they made us. Moreover, we notice that this is not just the past, but it continues into the present and waits for what we will make of it. We now sense that we have a choice between two alternatives, both of which the spiritual world enables us to realize. We can transform the enjoyments and the satisfaction we have received into a capacity to bring something into the world that, large or small, is valuable for the world. Alternatively, we can just take what we have received and enjoy it, in which case we incur a debt to the world and slowly suffocate spiritually, because we have not taken what we enjoyed as a reason to develop our capacity to bring something worthwhile into the world. Understanding this, we can live with the inner attitude that we cannot go through life merely enjoying what is given us; pleasure for ourselves is not enough. Unless gratitude becomes part of our feeling for life we cannot react in the right way. The transformation of pleasures of a purely spiritual nature is quite simple, but to transform enjoyments satisfied only through the body requires numerous incarnations, and between them we need to work repeatedly on such transformation. By pursuing egoistic enjoyment and the gratification of selfish desires we become debtors to the spiritual world.

When we enter the spiritual world, we notice in certain spiritual beings the fact that we have developed such debts. The pain they experience is so shocking and oppressive to the soul that it makes it difficult for us to prepare our next incarnation well and harmoniously. By contrast, pain, suffering, and grief that were truly lived through on Earth strengthen the soul and fill it with forces that become moral forces after death. This gives us the possibility in a subsequent life to develop our capacities to bring something of value into the world.

This and other experiences come to us directly after the midnight hour. We become aware of our current worth. Thanks to the existence behind us, we know what capacities we will possess in the future. After some time, we are given clear insight not just into our prior lives but also into the people who were connected with those lives, especially the closest connections. Throughout our time between death and the next birth, we have already felt community with those with whom we had close ties. When we meet them again after the midnight hour, the debts we owe to them clearly appear to them, just as their debts appear to us. We do not, as before, simply become aware of the nature of those relationships; these people now become the very expression of the settlement that is needed because of common past experiences. Through the people we now meet, we see what needs to happen in the coming life; we see how relationships from the past will have to be dealt with in the future. We receive insight into the spiritual "mechanics" of destiny, both in a personal sense and in our shared destiny with others. We see, for example, what we will have to do to avoid one-sidedness when we connect with communities of people, regardless of their nature.

The Human Ideal

The second part of our way through the planetary spheres also takes its course in the rhythmic breathing in and breathing out of spiritual social life and inner solitude, but it serves primarily to build up the spiritual archetype of our next incarnation. Long before we descend to the Earth, a spiritual–etheric archetype arises that pulls us down with spiritual, magnetic force toward the parents in whom we hope to find the desired hereditary factors. This occurs when we reunite with the fruits of our prior lives.

One thing is of great importance here: when our longing for an outside world is at its greatest, in the solitude of the midnight hour, the spirit transforms this longing into a kind of soul light. Until that time we have to preserve the connection with our "I," which is possible thanks to Christ, who guides us through the midnight hour. After this, the spirit can take over and guide us to our new life. If this does not happen, the power of Christ can lead us even beyond that point, although we then do not preserve a memory of ourselves.

If we had a strong bond with Christ during life on Earth, we find that, as a result, the spirit can work more powerfully in us on our way to Earth. We can then bring with us something from life before birth into earthly life, something that is not lost in the growing body. We then start life with a surplus of spirit that during life will enable us to recognize spirit.

Spiritual self-knowledge, which is destiny forming, is acquired by us when we constantly have the high ideal before us of our being human, which is the goal of the creative work of the gods. Grand and lofty, this ideal of our humanity, this goal of the gods, rises in spiritual distances. As we truly live into the second part of life between death and our next birth it acquires increasingly distinct contours.

These gods, whom we have come to know as the angels of the highest heavenly hierarchy, always have this ideal image of the human being before them as the image and likeness of divine being. In the world of spirit, the devotion of the gods is directed to this image, just as on Earth human beings worship what transcends humanity.* On Earth we might be nonreligious, even antireligious and want nothing to do with religion. In the world of spirit, no one is able to ignore this image of the human being; it always stands before us. Divine will and divine feeling flow into our will-permeated feeling and feeling-permeated will, giving us the strength to find our way to this image.

Initially, after going through the midnight hour, in our willing-permeated feeling and feeling-permeated will, out there in the widths of space we are still overcome by a kind of dullness in regard to this ideal image. Then divine powers begin to warm us inwardly so that we glow with enthusiasm. It is a kind of spiritual, religious instruction that speaks to our inner being

* Rudolf Steiner, *The Inner Nature of Man*, p. 37.

and causes us to gain the capacities to embark on our way to this ideal. We feel evermore closely connected with our hierarchical teachers; we feel strength growing in us as they help us.

During this divine instruction, we reach an important moment in our experience. The strength our divine teachers can instill in us depends on what we have made of ourselves in prior lives. We can approach the human ideal only to the extent of our inner ability.

Dangers of Spiritualization

Here we face a merciless test. The gods give us strength to the extent of our capacity, and now we would be able to become all spirit. We would then have to take all our imperfections with us into the spiritual world and, once there, get rid of them somehow. We can develop on the basis of what we have become in the meantime during all those lives. This means we have to let go of our ideal of being human; we have to become nonreligious, as it were, in the world of spirit.

The spirit that stands behind this test is Lucifer, who never had greater power over human beings than in this moment. He wants us to forget and ignore everything that is in us in principle but is not yet refined in the sense of that ideal. On our own, we would not be equal to this temptation, but the spiritual powers that Lucifer opposes lend a hand in this situation and fight with him for our soul. The result is that the archetypal image we had formed of our coming existence on Earth is cast out of time into space and is magnetically attracted, as it were, by spatial existence. At the same time, a kind of magnetic attraction arises from our future parents, and everything around us that could instill the temptation to remain in the spiritual world is removed from our view.

We begin to clothe ourselves in earthly physicality. This means we can then see the world of spiritual beings only from outside, no longer from inside. In the sensory world, spirits that foster development take us under their wing in soul depths, completely beyond our consciousness. Here we become aware of the fact that we need our earthly life in order to be removed from Lucifer's temptation. We may thank the spiritual powers that accompany us for their protection; they guard us so that we are not pulled during our life into tenuous spiritual spaces with all our imperfections.

We may thank the gods that they have left just as much consciousness to us on Earth as is good for us. We do have to realize, however, that this consciousness, particularly since the latter part of the twentieth century, has begun to open a crack into the suprasensory world. Spiritual experiences that were unheard of before now begin to enrich the lives of people, along with, however, all their concomitant dangers. The goal of the creative gods, which we viewed in the world of spirit from such a distance, can also be threatened on Earth when the inspirations that flow in through the cracks are received without sufficient consciousness. This could disturb the work of the divine beings working in our unconscious and guaranteeing our future.

We begin to have an inkling of this when we realize what happens in sensory perception. Whenever we make a perception something also happens in our unconscious being to the extent that the perception has entered beneath the skin and within the boundaries of the etheric body. Every sensory perception, every sensation we have can become conscious to us only if at the same time something dies in us. We are constantly taking the corpses and phantoms of our perceptions into us. How can that be?

Of all the many things we encounter, we are conscious of only a small part, about a fourth of it, the top layer. If our perception were complete, we would also open up the creative imagination, hidden behind the outer senses, containing inspiration and intuition. If these were to really penetrate us we would become so spiritual as to be incapable of resisting the temptation by Lucifer. On Earth, we would want to lead a tremendously spiritual life, to immediately become extremely spiritual; we would invade the spiritual world with all our imperfections, leaving our future-oriented capacities undeveloped.

Becoming an angel just-like-that without further preparation does not fit the intention of the world of spirit as in the "new and more perfect edition" envisaged by Benjamin Franklin. We need to work on ourselves for a very long time, on all the versions of ourselves that, as Franklin said, are to be "corrected and amended by the Author." It is good that we receive help so that we do not abandon the work.

9

Breathing in the Light

The light was always present for Jacques Lusseyran, but there were moments when it faded. This happened whenever he was afraid; fear made him blind. Anger and impatience had the same effect; they brought confusion. Jealousy and unkindness worked like fetters on the hands and feet, as if he were thrown into a dark pit. He was rewarded with light when he was happy and serene, and when he responded to people with confidence and good thoughts. "I saw the light, and I continued to see it, even though I was blind." This is how Jacques Lusseyran described his experiences after he became blind at the age of seven.*

As a very young child, he wasn't particularly interested in the Sun as it stood high in the afternoon. He constantly searched for its presence. He looked for it in the vibrations of its rays or in echoes—which we usually connect with sound rather than light—where the radiation is intensified, reflected from one window to another, from a wall to the clouds above. All of this permeated him, became part of him. "I ate the Sun," he wrote.

When he became blind he did not lose the light; this was his secret, about which he did not speak for years. It was always there, he bathed in it as in an element; in his blindness he had come much closer to it. He could feel how it welled up, dispersed, and rested on things, giving them form before it left them, diminishing, withdrawing—for there was never the opposite of light. Colors, too, all the colors of the rainbow, had

* Jacques Lusseyran (1924-1971), *And There Was Light.*

been preserved. People, things—everything had an individual, specific color.

He also discovered that everything in the world has a voice and speaks—the garden gate, the walls of houses, shadows thrown by trees, the sand, and stillness. He became aware of the way sounds do not begin or end abruptly; one can hear them almost before they are there. Sounds were of the same order as light, not inner or outer; they went through him. They helped him orient himself in his surroundings, brought him into contact with them, not as emitted signals but as answers. It was astonishing to discover that sounds never arose in a particular spot and never withdrew into themselves again. The sound was present, its echo, and a different sound with which the first one, having evoked it, would be fused—an infinite string of sounds.

In his contacts with the outer world, his hands had to become wise. He could no longer direct them to take hold of something; he had to let them do their own thing, gain their own experiences. Most of all, it was a matter of rhythm; the fingers had to learn to move and respond to things, which are all filled with life and ensouled, even stones. His fingers had to learn not only to feel the vibration, or knocking, in all they touched, but also to respond to it. When they did not do this, they lost their sense of touch. And pressure was even more important than movement; his fingers had to exert pressure, which was answered, and things came to meet him; they communicated. He entered a world in which everything is an exchange of pressure.

Slowly he also discovered that things are not fixed and enclosed within their forms. The air between the branches and leaves of the pear tree in the garden is part of the tree. When he walked along a road he knew exactly where the trees were, what kinds of trees they were, and the gestures their crowns made. They came to meet him as he moved on his way toward them.

With smell, things were just as they were with touch; there were physical smells and moral smells. This latter experience would stand him in good stead after the German invasion of France in 1940, when he started a resistance group with other young people. He became the gatekeeper for the group, the one who decided whether or not others could join them. He had a highly developed sense for the morality of others, which protected the group from betrayal from within. One day, however, his intuition faltered when the other person blocked his sense for the other. The candidate was given the benefit of the doubt and the traitor was let in.*

It is interesting to spend time with Lusseyran's autobiography and to read the whole book, trying especially to live into his experiences of light and sounds, the way he communicated through touch, and his direct moral insight into other people. In this way we come to know the world a little "from inside," a side that our senses do not usually reveal to us. This will help us when we try to imagine what we will experience through the transformation of our soul in the world in which it moves after death, "breathing in the light," as Christian Morgenstern put it.**

Breathing in the light—alternately breathing in during spiritual social life and breathing out during inner loneliness—we arrive in the world of our previous incarnations. The ideal of our humanity emerges deeply in the background, awaking self-knowledge that forms destiny. Our spiritual form adapted

* Jacques Lusseyran, *And There Was Light.*

** Christian Morgenstern, *We Have Found a Path.*

to the cosmos long ago by assuming the form of the Sun. On its path through the planetary spheres into the realm of the zodiac and beyond, the spiritual germs of its future organs are implanted into it. This has become possible because of two great changes; one caused the inner human being to become the outer, and the other sustained movement to transform the lower pole into the upper.

A transformation of soul forces prepares a subsequent change. We begin to form our next earthly existence according to our development of inner capacities in previous lives. What kinds of changes will result from our spiritual self-knowledge? How do the mechanics of destiny work?

Destiny Becomes Human

After the midnight hour of spiritual existence, we live in the outer world formed by the inner world of our prior lives. In the confrontation with this former destiny and seeing the human ideal in the background, we begin to work on our new destiny. I wrote in a previous chapter that, through the human beings we now meet, we perceive what needs to happen in the coming life; we recognize what the results of past relationships will have to be in the future. In a lecture cycle in 1914, Rudolf Steiner gave a few examples of how, through our encounters with others, destiny is formed in the light of the world of spirit.* The following is one example of many situations that form new destiny.

Suppose you once lied to a man. Each time you encounter that person (and you see him frequently before your spiritual eye) you are reminded in a painful way of how you twisted the truth to him. A predisposition now arises to meet that person again on Earth so you can compensate for what you caused

* Rudolf Steiner, *The Inner Nature of Man*, pp. 98ff.

with your lie, because it can become completely clear in the cosmos what you caused with it, and you have to set it right again on Earth.

This is just one example of many situations through which destiny is formed. Through such experiences we know that we need an earthly body to compensate for all our imperfections. Otherwise, those to whom we have become guilty in this way will continue to appear to us in our life between death and a subsequent birth to torment us, as reminders of the truth.

In the concrete process of forming our destiny after death—and destiny is always concrete—we are dealing not just with the heavenly hierarchies; there is also a great variety of elemental beings in the world where we then live. Thus far, they have been left out in my descriptions, but they must be mentioned here.

At this stage of preparation for a new life we might look back at the pleasures and joys we had and wish to transform those experiences. The fact that we want to do this, that we want to convert what we experienced into capacities, might annoy certain elemental beings, and they will want to prevent it. If we succumb to this, we risk losing our opportunity to set things right with others in the next life. If we decide to acquire those capacities anyway, such beings will give their frustrations free rein and send people who are possessed by them onto our path in the next life. This confronts us with a big problem in life: Should we let such people have their way or hinder their intentions? If we do not let them have their way, it may happen that the adversarial elemental beings at work in them take some kind of revenge for the fact that we have frustrated (or thwarted) them. But something like this could also end well for us. When we begin to consider such spiritual realities the world becomes complicated.

Consider the case of a girl who dies at a young age because of an illness. She takes forces with her that would otherwise have been fully used if she had lived into old age, but now she has a surplus of forces. These will strengthen her forces of will and feeling in the first part of her life after death. After the midnight hour, these forces can be used to strengthen the will in the next life. Those who commit suicide, however, will not possess such forces (see appendix 5). When people have a surplus of forces because they died in an accident, those forces become available to them after the midnight hour to strengthen their intellectual capacities. Brilliant inventors have often gone through such situations.

These are not the only kinds of experiences that demonstrate how differently we have to think when considering spiritual realities. For instance, people who die with a materialistic view of life have to suffer certain hardships after death if their loved ones who survive them also have the same worldview. If they, like the deceased, completely lack any spiritual inclination, they simply no longer exist for the deceased, as it were, and the deceased are unable to perceive them; their survivors are like a blind spot for them. However, the deceased do remember them from before their death. In their life after death the deceased have to wait until they have developed enough strength to realize *why* they cannot observe them. They then discover that those souls are living under the spell of Ahriman, the spirit who wants to nail everything down and deny all development. It takes great inner power to gain this kind of insight. With such survivors, the deceased can relate to them only after they have freed themselves from this spell after their own deaths.

Here's another example. Every human being receives the opportunity to come to Earth in a timely way, but this is often stymied so that most people begin their new lives much too early. This is especially true in the case of criminals, who are born too early in a spiritual sense. When we begin a new life too soon, we have not had the chance to connect with the body appropriately. Unconsciously, such people tend not to take life seriously. They have a strong urge for self-preservation and egoism, coupled with a kind of superficiality that prefers to dance through life.

It's not easy to come to terms with such remarks by Rudolf Steiner in the right way. Life between death and a new birth becomes extremely concrete if we have to consider the elemental beings and ahrimanic spirits that play an active role in the formation of destiny. It is certainly good to avoid the inclination to take such insights just as interesting factors that we can apply to ourselves and others. It is better to use them as reasons to familiarize ourselves with all that can play a role in the formation of destiny and make this part of our understanding of life.

This is extremely important, because we have become caught in abstraction upon abstraction ever since Rome invented the "citizen," a caricature of the true human being. In the city of Rome, for the first time in history, a human community was taken out of its natural environment. The city person arose and began to lead a separated existence; much later, citizens had no right to exist without their "papers." Even religious concepts—through which, in the far distant past, the human being was understood as a concrete microcosm within the macrocosm—got bogged down in Rome with legal frames of reference. For many of us, life after death has come to be seen as a simple continuation of life here on Earth and without a chance of essential change.

We see this embodied in the picture of St. Peter at the gate of heaven. He weighs us on his scale, giving us images of heavenly reward and punishment. Hardly any notion remains of something like turning inside out and downside up or other kinds of metamorphoses. Who among us can actually still connect with the great ideas of destiny from the ancient Greeks? Someone like Oedipus is completely incomprehensible when viewed through the lens of Roman legal concepts.

Visible Imaginations

Dealing in an appropriate way with examples such as these becomes even more important in yet another aspect of the mechanics of destiny. We find this in one of Steiner's lectures on karma in 1924.* He uses a number of examples to indicate how destiny manifests in the outer appearance of our human earthly figure, our physiognomy, or gestures. As human beings, we appear outwardly in many ways as the expression of our moral behavior in one or more prior lives on Earth, and we can discover mutual karmic connections in seemingly silly little things.

A couple of briefly described examples show how an inner disposition can express one's destiny. Such particulars will be hard to digest as long as we fail to realize how deeply we remain caught up in materialistic thinking. Doesn't heredity, upbringing, and the social factors where we grow up determine the person we are? It requires a clear inner step to acknowledge that we have made our own choices for the factors that help us to become human on Earth, that the circumstances in which we live are reflected in us. We can no longer take refuge in the idea that our destiny lives only as an inner reality in our encounters with others.

---

* Rudolf Steiner, *Karmic Relationships*, vol. 2, pp. 123ff.

What we see here is a special aspect of destiny formation—namely, our "destined constitution," the way we are built. But this is only one aspect of destiny; in every living human being we are dealing with someone who is carrying destiny created in the past, as well as new destiny created throughout the present life. We need to be well versed in this to distinguish how one is put together in this sense. For example, we meet attentive, observant people who are interested in everything they encounter. There are also people who feel at home in the past and have little notion of what happens in their own time and don't have much of a connection with daily life. Those who go through life with interest move easily, both inwardly and outwardly; such people reach out for things and want to get to know them. This has concrete consequences.

Recall that the lower pole of the previous life is transformed into the upper pole of the next life. We saw that we have to include in the lower pole everything that was not the head in the previous life, everything therefore that became physiognomy after the head had faded away in kamaloka. In a subsequent life the upper pole of such mobile individuals will tend to connect strongly with the forces of the Earth, especially in the embryonic phase through the first seven years, when the body is formed from the head. Such people will have large, strong bones, broad shoulders, and well-formed ribs. The forehead will not be high but well formed and striking. The hair will grow fast, especially in childhood. They will be intrepid, fearless people who do not flinch in the face of difficulties. On the other hand, those who never showed much interest in daily events in their previous life tend to become fearful and cowardly in the next life. Their upper pole has little connection with the Earth; their bones remain underdeveloped, they may have bowed legs or knobby knees, and their hair grows slowly.

The forces at work between death and a new birth are expressed in our constitution, and this is also partially true of forces from the previous life on Earth. Thus all sorts of aspects of our bodily constitution might be related to experiences in our previous life. However, it is not exactly useful, and might even be painful to others if we speculate on the ways this might apply to people around us. Nevertheless, it is good to realize that the inner realities of this life will become outer realities in the next.

Imagine, for example, a man who is a real thinker and frequently sits and ponders. He will be delicate and slightly built in the next life. Those who take things in hand, don't spend much time musing, and are generally energetic will tend to become stout in the next life. Meditating is not actually a requirement; rather, the point is to consider matters and have the will to make inner decisions. Real thinkers, regardless of profession or life situation, make much use of the upper pole, which fades away after death. Their skin, the body's surface, will be remarkably well formed with delicate flesh. Those who have spots on their skin and have trouble keeping it clean might have had little inclination to think and reflect in a prior life. Are there lots of freckles? Perhaps this person was not a deep thinker last time.

The point in these examples is to become aware of how the spirit works into matter; in the outer world, matter reveals spirit. The spirit works in imaginations in matter within the human body, and those imaginations appear in the form itself of the head, ears, nose, eyes, and in many other ways in our physique. As human beings, we consist of externally visible imaginations. But the kinds of imaginations these are in specific cases is something we should probably not go into.

Aftereffects

Previous examples give an impression of the mechanics of destiny to the extent that spiritual essence and morality are expressed physically in a subsequent life. The following example shows that the way a person moved through the world of spirit between death and the next life can become physically visible. In the middle area of the body, the experience of both the ascent to the midway point between death and rebirth and the subsequent descent come to expression. If we made the ascent quickly and the descent slowly and comfortably, the upper part of our trunk, between the neck and the middle of the chest, will be shorter than its lower part.

On the other hand, if we were slow and careful in the ascent and quick in descending to a new life, that relationship is reversed; the upper part of the trunk is longer than the lower part. In the first case, we need much more sleep than in the second, because we went rather carelessly through the previous life and subsequently had little interest in the first part of life after death. In the next life we evidently have to compensate for such a quick passage by sleeping a lot. In the second case, we were deeply engaged in life and had great interest in the ascent to the midnight hour; then we need less sleep in the next life.

There are also people who like to eat, whereas for others what's on their plate is unimportant. In life after death, this is expressed in the height to which we ascend. For those who eat to live, the midnight hour is much higher in the spiritual world; for those who live to eat, it is much lower.

In general, we can say that the amount of attention people give to their bodily existence reveals how they developed in their destiny since the previous life. Those who are overly delighted and enthusiastic eaters when they sit down to a meal were preoccupied with everyday matters in their prior life. They were content to move within generally accepted norms and customs. The language they spoke might also have contributed to this; a language whose sentence structure is prescribed precisely leaves little room for individual expression. It is not surprising that people who are forced to live in such restrictions of convention tend to become gluttons in their next life.

There are also ways that inner impulses can work through from one life to the next. There are people who are essentially serious; not that they are unable to laugh, but for them life is basically a serious affair. Others laugh with everything they do, even before they do it. In the first group, strong forces from the previous life are expressed: they have to take life seriously. When a previous life does not leave such strong aftereffects, perhaps a life lived in a semi-sleep state, we can be unable to go into the next life with sufficient earnestness and become someone who laughs too much or tells too many humorous stories.

Threefold Humanness

From these examples, we can see how in our humanness we become a reflection of the spiritual world in our destined constitution—in our figure, gestures, and the way we move. First, this comes to expression in our upper pole. In the head, we are essentially dependent on our prior lives; there we are unquestionably pictures of the world's imaginative element. Those who really want to study the human head need imaginative pictures. In our physical–sensory world, the head is the only thing for which we can use the imaginative pictures we need when we begin to perceive the spiritual world. In the spiritual world, spiritual beings first appear to us in pictures of a spiritual, etheric reflection. This happens when, like the seer of the Book of Revelation, we can climb up there, "lifted up to the world of spirit" (Rev. 1:10).

In the rhythmic system, it is more difficult to make such an observation. How does the breath work? How does the entire system come into movement? How does the breath reach the blood circulation? Through the blood circulation, for example, the breath is connected with thinking—which is highly refined "breathing"—and with movements of the limbs. In contrast to the head, the rhythmic system is in constant movement, always active, and we find there, on closer inspection, continual growth and decay, in which all four earthly elements (earth, water, air, and fire) are involved. We cannot understand the rhythmic system except in its continuous activity, in which the sensory transforms into the suprasensory, and the suprasensory again into the sensory. We encounter a musical disposition in this sensory reflection of the inspirational, sounding element in the world.

The lower pole of metabolism and limbs is all about the forces that work in it. To the extent it is visible to us, this system as a whole is actually an excretion product, of which the content of the intestines is only the most extreme example. This system is completely suprasensory, and we need to focus there on the spiritual impetus of the movements we can observe in the visible excretion products, such as hands and arms. As a suprasensory phenomenon within the physical world, the lower pole must be comprehended intuitively.

From the upper pole, which is a projection into the sensory world, we can learn the nature of imagination. From the rhythmic system, with its continual alternations between the sensory and the suprasensory, we can learn the nature of inspiration. Intuition can be learned from the suprasensory phenomenon represented in our world by the lower pole.

"Lifted up into the world of spirit," attempts to describe in words a condition in which we are "outside our self" but not the way this happens to people who become ecstatic through some violent emotion. The translator of the Book of Revelation tries to express that the author, the seer, was consciously able to observe an objective spiritual world outside his self. If words such as *rapture* or *ecstasy* had been chosen it would have suggested the subjective nuance of this being outside his self. The point is to transport our self mentally into a world where we can climb upward. For the steps of such a climb, Rudolf Steiner used the words *imagination, inspiration,* and *intuition.*

Imagination, Inspiration, and Intuition

These are Rudolf Steiner's technical terms for states of consciousness that transcend normal consciousness, our object-oriented consciousness wholly focused on the world that the senses open for us. As stages of suprasensory perceptive powers on the way to higher insight, although reachable for us during life only through arduous training, these states of consciousness become facts of life for the soul after death. *Imagination,* as a technical term, does not have the suggestion of imaginary, arbitrary, or haphazard, as usually attributed to the word, but refers to the fact that it has an image, or picture, at its core. It indicates a suprasensory reality clothed in pictures and transcending sensory observation. As a capacity, imagination enables us to learn about spiritual processes and how they change and transform into one another.

With the next higher step of suprasensory perception, *inspiration,* we come to know the expressions of spiritual beings at the level of soul. It enables us to penetrate their spiritual core and come to know their world as permeated by sounds. These beings reveal themselves there purely as sounds. As a technical term, inspiration is not about anything like in-breath, suggestion, or hunch, but has only to do with the element of sound common to such phenomena. Through inspiration, we begin to become aware of the music of the spheres.

Intuition, in this specialized language, is more than a mental picture or insight gained through inner vision, regardless of how it arose. With intuition we can transport ourselves mentally into the inner being of other entities—penetrate into them. Thus we can sense ourselves united with the objective spiritual world, while also remaining fully ourselves as individuals.

On the way toward insight, imagination enables us to experience observations no longer as external properties of beings, but recognize manifestations of inner spiritual reality in them. Inspiration brings us closer to the inner world of beings; it helps us understand what those beings mean to each other. With intuition, we penetrate the beings themselves.

After death we do this in a wholly natural way, depending on the capacities we gained in the previous life. "Breathing in the light" after the midnight hour of our spiritual existence, we return, from intuition to inspiration and imagination.

On our way into the world of spirit as we die, thoughts change immediately into pictures. We live for a long time with these pictures until they gradually change into the capacity of inspiration, and we perceive the harmony of the spheres. Ultimately, we grow to unite with the objective spiritual world, and then the soul becomes wholly intuition and one with the universe.

On the return journey from the midnight hour, we go in the reverse direction. The will—which had gone through the transformations on the ascent, as described earlier—returns as will; the intuiting soul is completely filled with it. It then reaches the conditions of inspiration and imagination. After a while it is ready to embody itself, and from the pictures of the imaginative condition in which it then lives, the upper pole for the next life comes into being. As it embodies itself, the soul again reaches the stage of thoughts that it left at death. We are then ready to begin our next life.

10

Heaven under Our Feet

Sometimes the stars seem far away; sometimes near and shining so clearly that we can distinctly see our feet throwing shadows. Under such a sky, we can almost pluck the stars. To walk under such a starry sky is a special experience. We meet the human being under the starry sky in Psalm 8:4, in which the question of the human being is asked, the mortal human being and the future human being.

> What is humankind that you are mindful of them,
> human beings, that you care for them?

We worked with this question at the beginning of chapter 5 and returned to it at the beginning of chapter 7 on the threefold human being. We did not consider then that the question is asked "under the starry sky."

> When I consider your heavens,
> the work of your fingers, the moon, and the stars,
> which you have set in place... (Psalm 8:3)

Who doesn't know the experience of everything seeming to fade away when we are absorbed in watching the starry sky at night? We forget ourselves and seem to merge into that shining world of stars far above us, the stars that nonetheless seem so close. We are completely surrounded by all those numberless star individualities up there. We see them in the part of the sky that is visible to us, but we know that they continue into the part we cannot see from our place on the Earth. We might then suddenly realize that we and the Earth on which we live are surrounded by worlds of star beings. We realize that as human beings on Earth we are never alone or abandoned, not as mortal human beings, nor as human beings focused on immortality. We experience duration and eternity.

By observing the heavens, the Moon and the stars, we receive a clear answer to the question of being human. The consciousness can grow of our little world that we are ourselves within the great world, our microcosm within the macrocosm, ourselves as spiritual beings amid countless spiritual beings. There, and there, and there—around all those stars are colonies of spiritual beings. Each star has them; suprasensory domains with their inhabitants exist everywhere, far beyond space and time. In the radiance of the stars, their domains enter our world. The sparkling stars above are only the outer indications of such colonies of spiritual beings; they signify the center of the active existence of the spiritual beings. The light that comes to meet us from the stars is a process within the beings that form those colonies.

When we let go of our etheric body after death and it dissolves, to be integrated into the elemental world, it expands into the starry world. As we have seen in previous chapters, we then grow into the secrets of the stars. On our passage through the far spaces of the cosmos, it becomes clear what we human beings really are—beings that are part of both the sensory and the suprasensory worlds.

Rudolf Steiner's Approach

We have seen that we can answer the question of the human being only "under the starry heavens." Now we can remember that we experienced a comparable moment when we realized that the development of the soul after death takes place in successive, interpenetrating planetary spheres. Our subject inevitably takes us into the cosmos.

It seems that Rudolf Steiner's descriptions of life between death and a next birth show us a clear line of development, which I have tried to follow in my descriptions. First, Steiner described the soul's existence after death in its experiences in the soul world, and subsequently that of the soul–spirit in the realms of spirit. He gave these descriptions at a time when he had to consider the concepts with which his theosophical listeners were familiar. (When Sukie Miller mentions Steiner, she is referring to that period [see page 16]). Although these concepts include the occult, from which many people shrink, they use patterns of thinking generally accepted in our culture today. It might require some extension of commonly used views and ideas, but it does not demand a radical change in the way we usually think. The development we find there is a direct continuation of earthly conditions. Essentially, these kinds of descriptions are not much different from those of the established churches, even if they don't get beyond Peter at the gate of heaven.

With the insight that the soul journeys through planetary spheres, Steiner then presented this development to a public that, with him, began to think anthroposophically and wanted to follow him in thinking into an objective cosmic world. During the same year, Steiner gave all of this a place in an objective spiritual world. At the time, he described experiences of the soul in the soul world after death as the result of its experiences with the destiny of the etheric body within the suprasensory world we know as the elemental world. He said something comparable about the spirit in the realm of spirits.

The uniqueness of Rudolf Steiner's insights into the life between death and a new birth really begins to show, it seems, with concepts such as "turning inside out" and "downside up," when he awakes us to the realization that we do indeed penetrate into another reality. Thus we are no longer surprised when he describes the inside becoming outside and the lower pole becoming the upper pole. These insights make it possible for us to follow the soul forces in their transformations that culminate in the midnight hour, which Steiner mentions for the first time in his fourth mystery drama. The first extensive description of these metamorphoses of the soul forces was given in his lecture series *The Inner Nature of Man: And Our Life between Death and Rebirth* in Vienna, April 1914. He referred often to these lectures later on.*

In our passages through the planetary spheres, experiences of the second part of our existence between death and rebirth reflect those of the first part. During the ascent and the subsequent descent, destiny is formed during periods of rhythmic alternations between a spiritual social life and inner loneliness. We can begin to follow the spiritual figure of the human being in the transformations that prepare it for a new embodiment. With the help of insight into physiognomy and with the picture of the threefold human being as a background, we see the human being developing as a spiritual, moral entity and growing into the world of the heavenly hierarchies.

Steiner's insights into existence between death and a new birth culminated in 1924, the last year he was still able to

* Between 1910 and 1913, Rudolf Steiner created four mystery dramas that depicted the experiences of people who sought their way toward "knowledge of higher worlds," each in their own individual way. The plays show the development of individuals who wrestle with their destinies within the context of their time.

lecture. His descriptions of the formation of karma were collected in eight volumes of more than eighty lectures.* In those lectures, the physiognomic aspect, which prepares for the new embodiment, is illustrated by examples to exemplify the mechanics of destiny. With the inner consistency of destiny as its basis, we also see how the destiny we will meet in the next life is worked through together with the spiritual hierarchies and ultimately modeled by the highest angels.

In the World of Stars

In the starry world that we see above us and know everywhere around us during life on Earth, many beings work hard on our future humanity as we make our way after death to a new life. In the process, we experience three aspects of our self. First, we realize how death ends our physical existence on Earth, while our physical remains are given over to the forces of nature to decay. This is the first aspect we experience of our self—death itself and the earthly aspect. When we view death through imagination, we see how human beings loosen themselves from the Earth at death as they rise from the dead body. From the moment of death, we are everywhere, not just where the body lies. We are indeed everywhere as we plunge with our suprasensory–physical body into the spiritual formative forces of the physical body (as described in the introduction). In this area of space, we enter a world of "cosmic thoughts."** We do not meet beings or gods there, as we might expect, but thoughts in the form of pictures.

* Rudolf Steiner, *Karmic Relationships*, vols. 1–8.

** See, for example, Rudolf Steiner, *Dying Earth and Living Cosmos*, March 5, 1918.

During these first days after dying we live in the sphere of cosmic intelligence. Our own life is taken up into it, and for a few days we have this before us in the tableau of our life. As this expands into the universe it becomes gradually more diffused until it eventually fades away. This is a fearful moment: *Will I, too, fade away with my life into the universe?* Here we find the second aspect of ourselves—the dissolution of our self with our earthly life, the spatial aspect. However, this is the point where we can no longer perceive with an imaginative capacity. We experience what happens after those first few days only through inspiration. We begin to take up thoughts without needing the help of pictures. We begin to hear spiritually; we hear the cosmic word sounding clearly from all sides; we hear spiritual speech.

Finally, through the capacity of intuition, we become aware of the beings speaking behind those thoughts. This is the third aspect of ourself that we experience at the boundary of the universe visible to our ordinary sight. Through intuition, we perceive the stars as revelations of beings; we see colonies of spiritual beings in lieu of stars. We feel how the world of the stars takes us human beings into itself; we see how we become heavenly beings among heavenly beings.

However, the starry world that is spread out above us is not a homogeneous world. Among the spiritual beings who form our solar system, there are angels who want to be autonomous and want their own inner life. They rally around Lucifer, the spirit who sows confusion everywhere; to be independent, they have to become rebels in the hierarchical order, spirits of untruth and lies, who disavow their own essential being. They won their independence in the solar system by closing themselves off, and this has had far-reaching consequences for our planetary system.

In chapter 2 we became acquainted with the planetary spheres, in which the planets mark the extent, so to speak, of their spheres through their orbits. We have to imagine that everything within that space is filled with the etheric substance of that planet, the orbit of which marks the boundary of its sphere. We also saw that the nine angelic realms are expressed in the planetary spheres. The spiritual beings of our solar system find their common center in the Sun. From the Sun, their forces work outward to create the planetary spheres. If they were the only beings at work in the universe, the planets would consist of what we now recognize as their spheres; each planet would coincide with its etheric sphere.

The rebelling spirits work against the planetary spirits through their centrifugal forces. Because of their activity, an abnormality develops at the outer boundary of the etheric planetary sphere, a kind of "dent" that is closed off. We see this as the visible, physical planet, where a force field exists in which two opposing forces meet; the normal planetary forces that emanate from the Sun encounter those of the luciferic spirits working abnormally. Viewed spiritually, this "dent" is a hole in the universe; where we see a planet in the sky is exactly the place where it is absent etherically. Through the collision of these two opposing forces, the form of the etheric substance is shattered. The form is splintered, and we know this shattered form as matter.

In the same way, the planets also become bearers of light; the centrifugal forces of light collide with the abnormally working forces of the luciferic spirits. The activity of these spirits—who do not want only to be themselves but also to claim their light for themselves—causes the light that emanates from the Sun to be caught and reflected back. Lucifer is indeed the original lightbearer, the one who makes light physical and visible.

Threefold Destiny Formation

We live alternately on Earth under the starry skies and then in the starry skies themselves to form our destiny. The Earth is the place where we meet our destiny, where we prepare new destiny through our thoughts, words, and deeds. However, the stars (i.e., the beings manifestly present in the stars) transform what is thus prepared into the destiny of our next life. Work on this transformation begins with the souls of planetary spirits we meet before the Sun sphere, and this continues into the spheres of the outer planets, Mars, Jupiter, and Saturn. During the ascent, the first fundamental form of the coming physical embodiment is developed in our first sojourn in the Sun sphere. In the second sojourn in the Sun sphere, during the descent, it is more the beginning of our future moral existence that is formed.

The cosmic ether—to which the etheric body was surrendered at the beginning of the ascent and gradually integrated into it—is invisible and suprasensory, as is our own etheric body. At its boundaries, however, we are indeed able to perceive the cosmic ether. The majesty of the ether reveals itself in the blue of the heavens, and there the invisible comes (just barely) within our reach. The next world, which is also suprasensory, is immediately perceptible in the astral aspect of the cosmos, which shines into our world through every star. The cosmic suprasensory astral becomes visible in this wondrous mass of lights that, alone or in groups, send down their influence, not unlike someone gently caressing another's cheek.

The last and fourth world, suprasensory and purely cosmic, is that of the beings behind these light rays, the caresses of the etheric world. It is the world of those angels with whom human beings give new form to their destiny; it is a purely inner process that takes place wholly in time, with absolutely no spatial component.

Thanks in part to the various hierarchies, during our life on Earth we are connected in many different ways with the world around us. Some of this happens consciously, such as in our mental pictures of things, and some unconsciously, as in our respiration and metabolism. In part of our upper pole, our seat of thinking, we are connected with the third hierarchy, the Angels, Archangels, and Archai. In the middle area, the home of our dreamlike feeling life, we are connected with the second hierarchy, the Exousiai, Dynamis, and Kyriotetes, whom we carry "in our chest" as the place of their activities in us. The first hierarchy—the Thrones, Cherubim, and Seraphim—works in the lower pole of metabolism and movement. There is a continuous process of combustion and breakdown in this lower pole, where we absorb the spiritual essence of substances we take in from the outer world. In the lower pole, therefore, the first hierarchy connects us with what fills us with spirit.

What do these angels of the various hierarchies do in us? The third hierarchy has to do with our thinking. They forge the link between observation and recollection and guarantee memory in our upper pole; in this domain, which lies outside our consciousness, they lead us through life. After dying, we awake to the suprasensory world in their region. We find the angels of the second hierarchy after death in the level below it—in the perceptible supraphysical world. With them, we work out our destiny for the next life, which will be expressed in our bodily constitution. As we penetrate more deeply into life after death, we become aware of the angels of the first hierarchy in the invisible physical world.*

Indeed, while we are living on Earth we look for the highest gods "up there in heaven," but in our life between death and a

* See Rudolf Steiner, *Death as Metamorphosis of Life,* "What Does the Angel Do in Our Astral Body?" (Oct. 9, 1918).

new birth we have to look for the highest, but still accessible, divine beings far below us. The angels of the first hierarchy, the creative gods of our universe, have the task of reproducing for us everything we have done as human beings during life. They do this in a very particular way; they have to create the exact likeness of all we have done on Earth, both good and bad. While we are working with the second hierarchy on inner progress, the inner consequences of our destiny, we observe what the Thrones, Cherubim, and Seraphim have experienced in our earthly activity. Below us we observe the heavens formed by their work, in the likenesses they create, settling and balancing equitably and justly all that human beings have done on Earth. Everyone views the consequences of their own deeds and omissions individually in the actions of the gods.

The inner consequences of our destiny are expressed in our bodily organism. We also take them with us as talents, proficiencies, and shortcomings. What the gods have made in heaven under our feet, what they had to go through because of our earthly life, comes to meet us in the next life as facts that determine our destiny.

Freedom and Necessity

One could say that we are "fully present" on Earth only when making use of sensory perception and the intellect. As human beings we are filled with the third hierarchy in our upper pole, filled with the second hierarchy in the ground of our feeling, and filled with the first hierarchy of angels in everything related to the will. This means that we always live within the world of the hierarchies, and rise above it only through our senses and intellect—a little like swimming with only our head above the water. Consequently, the hierarchies can use us as organs of perception. We are not only dwelling places for the gods, we are also their eyes, with which they can perceive the cosmos.*

Therefore, in all that we do in ordinary consciousness, we are free; we are not the subjects of or dependent on the angels in what we create with our sensory perceptions and intellect. We find the physiological basis of our freedom in this phenomenon. We form our destiny with the gods who live in us; countless beings work with us to form our destiny. As a result, necessity is a factor in destiny, so people tend to feel that destiny is fate, from which it is impossible to escape, but that is just a deceptive appearance. The inevitability of destiny applies only to the circumstances—the facts served up by destiny—and not to the way we deal with and react to those facts and circumstances. We can, certainly, resign ourselves to our perceived destiny; it is also a free deed not to resist—to renounce dealing creatively with what is dished out by destiny. The destiny we formed with the hierarchies constantly places us at forks in the road. We have to choose, to decide among the various possibilities offered to us. Although we often fail to notice that we do indeed make such choices, this does not change the fact that we are free, in every moment of destiny in our life, when we make choices.

Rudolf Steiner explains that the cosmos in which destiny is created with this inevitability is threefold, consisting of physical, etheric, and astral worlds. In our physicality, our nature is the same as these worlds in physical, etheric, and, astral respects. But our "I," the bearer of our destiny, stands outside those worlds, though it alternates between the physical plane during life and the astral plane between death and a new birth. The etheric, elemental world has no significance for the "I,"

* Rudolf Steiner, *Karmic Relationships*, vol. 2, p. 208.

because the etheric body is surrendered to this world only a few days after death. This means that the angels of the third hierarchy receive our web of destiny; they breathe in the thoughts of the deceased. At that point, we can begin to process the life that has just ended; it then stands in its totality before the soul, as if from without, just as it was experienced by others.

In contrast to the etheric world, the astral world, which shines into us through the stars, does have significance for the "I" between death and a next birth. This is the world of the angels of the second hierarchy, through whom destiny becomes a cosmic reality.

We cannot follow the "I" from incarnation to incarnation unless we leave space and plunge into the stream of pure time. To experience time as a reality, we have to die, since during life on Earth we always experience time through spatial, physical circumstances. After leaving the physical world, the "I" comes, via the etheric and the astral world, to a true "supraearthly" world. The "I" has its home in this world, which expresses itself through cosmic astrality and is a world of beings and spirit that rests only in itself. There it finds "heaven under its feet."

The Cosmic Human Being

During life between death and a next birth (Steiner repeatedly points this out), nothing we call "us" is enclosed within anything like a skin, but is external to us; the world we experienced outside on Earth is now within. If we want to understand our existence in the Sun sphere we have to realize that everything we call the world on Earth is now within us—the Moon, Mercury, Venus, even the Sun sphere in its totality, which is pure goodness, where no evil has access. In the Sun sphere, just as on Earth, we can distinguish between something like our head and the rest of our body. There, we can say that the Moon, Mercury, and Venus become our limbs; the Sun itself, with all its beings, becomes our whole rhythmic system with heart and lungs.

Mars, Jupiter, and Saturn are, so to speak, our head—our organ of knowledge and insight. Just as on Earth we need the lower part of our head in order to speak, now we live by means of the cosmic word, because we have Mars in us. Just as we walk around on Earth with thoughts and memory, on Jupiter we bear cosmic wisdom in us; and cosmic memory on Saturn. What we observe outside us, which becomes "our world," is the spiritual human being who is as great and majestic as the universe itself with all its stars. Indeed, all the heavenly hierarchies, which are hidden but present in us during life on Earth, are our outside world in Sun existence.

Living in the beholding of the miracle that human physicality is spiritual, we are working with the angels of the third and second hierarchies on our next life, especially on the future earthly human being, during our first sojourn in the Sun sphere. If in this phase the work on the future human being were already completed, we would already all have become angelic beings, full of goodness and on the verge of being gods—but without freedom and without being able to choose between good and evil. After the midnight hour, therefore, in the second part of the Sun existence, during our descent, this primordial form of our future humanity is transformed.

Part of it remains a spiritual reality; another part fades away and becomes a reflection. The spiritually real part becomes the beginning form for the rest of the body; the part that is a mere reflection of reality becomes the basis of the head. Based on its "reality-as-reflection," this part can take more compact matter into the skull on Earth, but in the beginning form of the human being in Sun existence it is open for the germ of later personal morality. In the coming life, this part—which has not become a complete reality—guarantees our freedom.

In this second part of life between death and a next birth, the Thrones, Cherubim, and Seraphim no longer appear in what had been the macrocosm within us, but in a suprasensory world outside us. In the spheres of Mars, Jupiter, and Saturn, where they are active, the suprasensory world they create for us appears under our feet. Then, above us is the vault, as it were, of the pure realm of spirit, and below we see our coming destiny taking form as acts of the gods and as the fulfillment of destiny from our past life. We have yet to investigate whether or not this is the form of the destiny that will await us on Earth.

11

The Destiny that Awaits Us

Once we begin our descent toward the Earth after the midnight hour, we leave the world of the Thrones, Cherubim, and Seraphim. Then the web of our coming destiny appears to us in a heaven under our feet, above which stretches the vault of the actual world of spirit, in all that the beings of the first heavenly hierarchy have been able to create for us from our prior sojourns on Earth. In the details that determine our coming destiny, we see spread before us what they have experienced as the necessary consequences of our actions in our last life; those results reach the Earth like a gentle rain. Everything that comes to meet us as our destiny is a reflection of what the gods have arranged for us—whether we meet someone who has a decisive influence on our destiny, whether we end up in a place that becomes important for us, or whether we enter a particular profession.

In the image of rain and snow falling from the heavens to moisten the Earth, ancient peoples recognized the direct influences of the divine world on instances of human destiny. The second part of the book of Isaiah offers a marvelous picture of this:

> As the rain and the snow
>   come down from heaven,
> and do not return to it
>   without watering the earth
> and making it bud and flourish,

> so that it yields seed for the sower and bread
> for the eater,
> so is my word that goes out from my mouth:
> It will not return to me empty,
> but will accomplish what I desire
> and achieve the purpose for which I sent it.
> (Is. 55:10–11)

The Lord, the God of this people, adds:

> You will go out in joy
> and be led forth in peace;
> the mountains and hills
> will burst into song before you,
> and all the trees of the field
> will clap their hands. (Is. 55:12)

What a reception for those who go forth, guided and carried by their God! A heartwarming picture and a wonderful prospect also for those beginning a new incarnation on Earth and the web of destiny they find there; they know that their God remains close to them in their lives and actions. In Isaiah, the Old Testament still spoke of the one God, who "shall have no other gods before me" (Ex. 20:3). Christianity has, in the meantime, come to view the heavenly hosts in their fullness as the servants of the Triune God. After a life of joys and suffering, battles and peace, the word of the angels that formed human destiny will not return to them empty. They remain connected with the destiny of their human charges.

Rudolf Steiner used the depiction in the book of Isaiah when he described what we experience after death when we return to the realm of angels in kamaloka; there we are turned inside out in the transition from the sensory world to the suprasensory world. We are inwardly prepared for this experience in the first days that follow death, when we experience a review of our life in the tableau of memories that rises before us.

The Work of the Angels

Most of the mental pictures we carry with us in life are related to our experiences and perhaps to the significance of our deeds for another person. We tend to lack any notion of the reality of our actions for the spiritual world—how a good deed awakes soul warmth there, a bad one awakes coldness, and how other deeds cause bright radiance or darkness; such results of our actions pass us by on Earth. We can become aware of them only through imagination, but we do experience them subconsciously—that is, we actually experience the effect of our good deed or our misdeed in the spiritual world.

Once we have learned to recognize this, we become aware of the fact that our experiences are really one-sided and imperfect. In our life panorama, which reaches back to birth or even earlier, we will therefore feel that we have missed quite a lot; we might feel as if we went through life handicapped or damaged. We were blind to the spiritual dimension of our existence and have thus incurred a debt to the world. Nonetheless, we have to let that debt stand, because we cannot do anything about it until after death. It's as if we have incurred debts throughout life that we can never repay. Returning to the image of the door in chapter 5, we have been unable to fill the holes in the door.

It is with this kind of realization that we enter kamaloka in the right way, so that we are able to experience what we left unfinished during life by *not* experiencing it. Thus we review our life now without focusing on what our deeds meant to us. We are in a kind of embryonic state in regard to the universe as we go through the effects of our actions for the world. At this stage we are still connected with the Earth—not carried by a mother but by all that we did *not* experience.

With a strong feeling of our own smallness, we become aware of the exalted beings far above us who manifest sympathy or antipathy for our experiences as we go through our life in reverse. As we live through the spiritual side of our earthly activities, this sympathy and antipathy trickles down on us like a soft rain. We feel how what becomes saturated in sympathy can be taken up in the universe and will become a good contribution, whereas everything on which antipathy trickles down is rejected as harmful to the universe, which is why we cannot hand it over but have to keep it with us until it is offset by later actions. In this way, we lay the foundation for the destiny of our next life.

Each time we are turned inside out or downside up, so that we can enter another kind of existence, the angels help us adapt to the web of destiny in our new situation. They offer examples of what was prepared spiritually between death and the next birth, so that our destiny can become reality on Earth. Moreover, they can take up the eternal value contained in our destiny into their worlds, but the influence of the angels in destiny goes even beyond this.

We can clearly discover two different aspects of destiny through the ways we come into contact with others. One connection is deeply anchored in our own destiny; we meet those with whom we had a connection in prior lives, such as relatives or others who played a role in our life, in accordance with the way we prepared it with them after our death, and in the way it resulted from previously existing destiny. However, we are born into a specific people and in a specific place on the

Earth. The cause of this certainly lay in our own destiny, which searched for forms in which it could be realized.

But we also participate for a while with those with whom we had no previous destiny—for example, in various social and spiritual communities. Consider all the people with whom we were together in school and our contacts in clubs, a church, or other organizations. Such contacts do not arise from connections in prior lives but are based on what was created between death and the next birth. The gods who prepare the web of our destiny weave this into that of various groups of people. Spiritual and cultural life, as well as shared destiny with people of a particular language or ethnicity on Earth, are prepared in this way during our pre-birth existence.

What the gods do for the individual human being at the beginning and end of life they also do for those who share a common destiny on Earth. The angels of the first hierarchy are directly involved with their own actions in everything that happens on Earth as collaborations among people in shared thinking, experiencing, feeling, and acting. What people thus experience together flows into the actions of these angels, who show us the consequences of this as examples, just as they do for the web of our personal destiny.

The metamorphosis of what people go through together comes down like a soft rain thirty to fifty years later and permeates the souls of those who are living. This is why we might occasionally notice how certain people and their deeds in a relatively recent past seem to be close to us spiritually, which might not always happen in a favorable way. This is often connected with specters from a prior time—ghosts still hanging in the air from stereotypical views and feelings that were generally accepted at the time.

Causes and Their Effects

In the destiny that softly trickles down, we recognize one of its aspects. Through the idea of cause and effect, can we become more familiar with the circumstances and laws that govern the formation of destiny? It is interesting to review how Rudolf Steiner spoke of cause and effect in the kingdoms of nature. He said that we can look at lifeless nature for the causes of what happens in the lifeless itself. This is true, too, for a dead body, which immediately begins to change chemically and physically once the living body becomes a corpse. All kinds of changes continuously occur in water and air, too. We find that cause and effect occur simultaneously in the mineral world. The effects show insofar as the causes exist; when the causes disappear, the effects are also gone. For all that happens in the domain of lifeless things, we can find causes that are active at the same time.

In the plant kingdom, phenomena take place for which we also have to look for causes at the same moment in time. Here, however, we have to call on the aid of the universe, since we have to find the causes in another realm, the etheric world. We human beings participate in this with our etheric body, and although it takes a few days for the etheric body to be released and to complete its integration into the elemental world, we can also speak of "concurrence." There is simultaneity of cause and effect in this realm—causes in the supraphysical and effects in the physical.

When it comes to animals, we do not find simultaneous causes for typical elements such as movement and moods. For this we have to look back to what precedes life itself and underlies life, back to the starry constellations of the past. In human beings, we find those laws after death, when we have gone back through our life in the astral body to before our birth. In the animal kingdom, effects in the present have supraphysical causes in the past. To find causes in this realm, we have to leave space and go back in time.

For typically human aspects, causes also lie in the past; we find physical causes in the past for physical effects in the present. Steiner made this understandable by reminding us that a line going to the right into infinity returns from the left.

In these four cases in the kingdoms of nature, we encounter a lawfulness similar to that in the four realms we learned about as our worlds. We saw in the physical and supraphysical worlds a contrast between visible and invisible. Here, however, we have a contrast in time. With the help of these insights we can find a reflection of the four worlds in the kingdoms of nature:

1. The mineral realm is the reflection of a visible, physical world; in it we find simultaneity of cause and effect in the physical.
2. In the plant kingdom we witness an expression of an invisible, suprasensory world and simultaneity; however, the cause here lies in the suprasensory and its effect in the physical.
3. In the animal kingdom, a visible suprasensory world appears; effects in this realm arise from suprasensory causes in the past.
4. The human kingdom makes an invisible, physical world visible; regarding physical effects, we find their physical causes in the past.

Destiny Formation during Life

Now, what does this mean for the destiny that awaits us on Earth? We have contact with the lifeless mineral realm mostly through our senses; a little in our food through salt, for example. We can move freely and independently in the mineral realm, and eventually we leave a corpse behind in it.

However, there is no freedom in the world of plants; in the etheric realm we participate in many kinds of life phenomena on which we depend completely. We depend equally on the spiritual realm behind the elemental world (angels of the third hierarchy) to maintain the plant kingdom. With the help of etheric forces, they form the constitution of our destiny, expressed in our physical constitution, such as good health and wellbeing, as well as inner discomfort and illness. We form our etheric body with these angels during the last phase of our sojourn in the suprasensory worlds.

Sympathies and antipathies are aspects that work deeply into destiny. Like the animals, we are influenced in our astral body by the places on Earth where specific animal forms manifest. These feelings radiate to a greater or lesser extent and give us the opportunity to become world citizens or to remain fettered to our own little piece of clay. Such sympathies and antipathies go out to other peoples, nations, and races, for example, as well as to a myriad of artistic and cultural expressions. Such inborn feelings, the nature of our destiny, we owe to the angels of the second hierarchy. Based on what they have imprinted in us, we look for our future parents and the elements of heredity we need.

Of course, the most profound influence on our destiny comes from the human realm itself. All human interactions meet us in life through the karmic web of events and experiences that give our life form. As we saw previously in this chapter, the angels of the first hierarchy are active in this way. The "I" that passes from life to life lives in this realm.

Thus we see that our destiny has three aspects. We meet the first one in the facts of our life woven into the *web of destiny.* We recognize the second aspect in the *nature of our destiny;* this is the way we meet what awaits us, our instincts and predispositions. The third aspect is in our *destiny constitution*, which determines how we "are put together" and how we experience ourselves in our physical constitution, our threefold humanness. In chapter 9 are several examples of the formative power of the mechanics of destiny, in which the destiny constitution is expressed.

The web of our destiny reaches the Earth like a soft rain. Rudolf Steiner used this image to express the fact that on the Earth we get under our feet, as it were, what we saw in the "heaven under our feet" during our descent to Earth. Behind this image is the fact that the angels of the first hierarchy are also involved directly in our destiny during life.

The angels of the third hierarchy stand, so to speak, at our cradle. They help us with the development of our senses and intellect, among other things; thus they assist the soul in the process of incarnation. The inhabitants of the spheres of Mars, Jupiter, and Saturn provide the forces they need for this. They observe human beings on their descent through the spheres and notice what they lack—namely, what the cosmos found unusable in us and thus had to be left behind in the lower planetary spheres. We entered the Sun sphere in a crippled state, and the inhabitants of the higher planetary spheres satisfied the demands of our future destiny based on those mutilations. They communicated this to the angels of the third hierarchy, who imprinted it into the spiritual foundation of our nerve–sense system, centered in the head and spread throughout the body. Unconsciously to us, this takes place during our first twenty-one years, the period of life when destiny states its demands.

Later, the Seraphim, Cherubim, and Thrones (the inhabitants of Saturn, Jupiter, and Mars) become active in our lower pole. This happens to us, again completely unconsciously, in the phase of life between our twenty-eighth and forty-ninth years, when the fulfillment of our destiny is growing. They have to remind us that whatever remains unfulfilled will be preserved for the next life.

Whatever we experience, consciously or unconsciously, influences our destiny. Sleep is critically important in this sense. When we fall asleep, the astral body and the "I" separate from the physical and etheric bodies. They move out through the nerve–sense system, primarily through the head, but in a certain sense also from the whole body that remains behind. The "I," which is somewhat larger, surrounds the astral body.

When we awake the astral body returns through the tips of our fingers and toes, and the "I" comes with it, "enclosed" within the astral body. Together they need the whole day to spread through our physicality, and once they reach the head we are ready to leave the body again.

Throughout our life, therefore, the "I" and astral body are in continuous, flowing movement—that is, the members of our being, for which we are accustomed to using those terms. As we have seen, during life we are dealing with reflections of the real "I" and astral body, both of which remain behind in pre-birth existence.

This gradual penetration into physicality has the effect that our astral body and "I" do not reach all the way to our wrists and ankles until about a half hour after we awake. Why, then, doesn't it take us the whole day to wake up completely? Well, even when the astral body has only just taken possession of our fingertips and toes, it can already work within the whole body. Although it spreads through the body slowly, its effect is present from the beginning.

As the astral body and "I" leave the body, the formation of destiny begins immediately, albeit in a pictorial form. The experiences of the day are transformed so that they can form part of the developing destiny. In a later stage of sleep, we are also submerged in the experiences of our previous life and, following that, in those of the life before that—and we continue to go back. When we awake we have passed our first individual life, and even all that belongs to the time before we led our own individual life, when we were still part of the life of the universe. All of this also happens, though briefly, when we take a short nap. Thus, each time we sleep we have an opportunity to meet our destiny.

Our Incarnations

Our experiences during sleep that become part of our destiny take place in the small fragment of the world that has become "our world." This fragment of the world lends a strong color to our destiny, but (and this is its spiritual side) it has been given to us by the angels who form and accompany our destiny. In "our" part of the world, therefore, only the destiny that the first hierarchy has shown us cosmically rains down. During the preparation for our incarnation, this piece of the world was chosen for us. What does this mean?

As a general rule, we always return to the Earth after conditions there have changed profoundly. Rudolf Steiner connects this with the precession of the equinoxes—the point where the heavenly equator intersects with the ecliptic. The spring equinox moves through all the signs of the zodiac in the course of centuries, taking 25,920 years to complete this orbit, the time called a *platonic year.* The time it takes for the equinox to pass through one sign is typically 2,160 years. In its course through the zodiac, the Earth continuously receives new impressions from the cosmos. As human beings, we want to participate in this, so within a period of 2,160 years, we will want to have at least one incarnation.* Actually, we want at least two incarnations in each period—one as a woman and one as a man.

Whereas the time between incarnations is determined by cosmic factors, the place depends partially on "soul migration," a movement from West to East across the face of the Earth. In the sequence of cultures, we can observe a movement from East to West, from ancient Asia via the Middle East and Near East to the areas around the Mediterranean and up into the heart of Europe. The movement of human beings who look for subsequent incarnations goes in the other direction; therefore, we do not move with our culture.

In the first decades of the twentieth century, when Rudolf Steiner was lecturing, there were many people in western Europe who had lived in their previous life on the American continent during the European conquests there. Those who had lived through the expansion of Christendom from southern to northern Europe had moved, after a longer interval between their incarnations, to Asia, particularly Japan. Asiatic souls appeared on Earth in North America.

---

* Rudolf Steiner, *The Temple Legend,* Oct. 21, 1905; Steiner spoke of periods of 2,000 to 3,000 years between two "full" incarnations; perhaps he referred here to the larger signs that occupy more than a twelfth of the zodiac; see also *Rosicrucian Wisdom,* p. 51.

When observing this movement, we should not forget that physical bodies everywhere on Earth have a "local past"; they have been subject to local influences for centuries. These physical bodies are claimed by souls that had a completely different past in their prior incarnation. They migrate to a different situation to gain new experiences. This is the only real soul migration.

In these examples, the indigenous peoples who perished in the Americas were an exception to the general rule that there should be 1,000 to 1,100 years between incarnations. In Steiner's descriptions of the destiny of people through several incarnations (such as those included in the *Karmic Relationships* lectures), we are often struck by the particulars of the unique ways that destiny works. A few of these follow below.

Most Individual Content

It was just noted that two incarnations belong together, and this brings us to another law—that some incarnations are more important for the development of destiny than others. There are incarnations that have critical importance for a developing individuality and determine destiny in a decisive way. There might be an unimportant, perhaps short, incarnation between two more important ones. In the past, such in-between incarnations usually took place in a female body, because traditionally women had fewer opportunities than men to develop their individuality. Men could more easily acquire certain positions of importance. In the meantime, this has changed radically; in the future, female incarnations will have exceptional importance. Steiner described such an exception with great emphasis.* This was a female, in-between

* See Steiner's lecture of Apr. 9, 1924. An important exception to this law is mentioned in the lectures of Apr. 16 and 23, 1924; all three lectures are included in *Karmic Relationships*, vol. 2.

incarnation that had great importance for the person, because the individuality was able to make subtle observations of events around her that would have been far more difficult in a male body. In another example, Steiner discussed a series of incarnations and pointed out how experiences from a former life were lived through again in a female incarnation, but now not so much through the forces of the head but anchored deeply in the heart.*

However, incarnations that take place in the limelight (usually men in the past) are not always the best. In more recent centuries especially, people who are destined to hold positions of power in one incarnation return after a very short interval. Oliver Cromwell is a good example. Steiner said in this regard that it was often a selection of the worst that enabled people to obtain such positions of power. Through their brief sojourn in the world of spirit, such people absorbed very little spirit and were correspondingly more strongly inclined to the Earth.** As we have seen, they share this destiny with criminals.

Whenever we come back, we find ourselves in the midst of a group of people who belong together. People incarnate rhythmically, in groups, so that we repeatedly meet "our own people" and are contemporaries of one another. We repeatedly meet some of these people personally, whereas we come to know others only from history. We do not always encounter the latter, and one aspect of this is certainly the fact that we can better evaluate a person we have never met and never will. In this way, we are not distracted by all kinds of interfering personal traits; we can better appreciate such a person without prejudice based

* Ibid., May 29, 1924.

** Rudolf Steiner, *Understanding Society through Spiritual-Scientific Knowledge*, Oct. 12, 1919.

on prestige and personality. Of course, people who thus fail to meet each other in life might still come together in the much longer life between death and the next birth. People who share many experiences in one life might not always meet in the next. Individually, they have the potential to realize common intentions in life, even though they might not incarnate again at the same time.

Moreover, we should not forget that the person we are is much more a product of our environment than we tend to admit. Upbringing, education, and the contemporary social milieu put a distinct stamp on us. We are not always easily recognized in that kind of "packaging." However, this is also the way it is with people we have not seen for years; often, we finally recognize each other through a characteristic gesture, a way of walking, a hand movement, or a way of holding the head. We reveal ourselves in largely unconscious small ways and in the manner that we react to people and things that cross our path.

There are those who always begin by rejecting things, and hesitantly give in only after someone insists; others immediately embrace what life puts on their plate, but then have trouble taking a position. It is such habits and gestures that give us the feeling of really getting to know and seeing people through their usual way of standing in life, without the ballast of a temporary "package." Thus, the "I," which passes from incarnation to incarnation, remains the same in one's life gestures.

The whole area of human relationships is astoundingly complicated. The fact that we and another might be like fire and water to each other and negatively influence each other is often based only on the fact that we can be incredibly irritated by some tiresome habit in the other. Something like this can arise spontaneously and only now become a factor in destiny, with its consequences occurring in a subsequent life. It might also be something that has existed between us from far in the past, even before the time we spent together preceding this life, whereas we fully penetrated each other in our passage through the spiritual world. We can try to develop a sense for such different possibilities. For some people, contact is easy and spontaneous, but for those who like to remain in the background, it may take a long while before they begin to mean something to us. Maybe this is precisely because we have a long history together; such a relationship might exist inconspicuously and quietly for years and then suddenly have great significance.

In all that trickles down to Earth as the web of destiny, we find "heaven under our feet" in a direct sense—that is, a common destiny in which we try to find our way. For the prophet Isaiah, an image for the way God's Word works is the experience of rain and snow descending from the heights and moistening the Earth to provide nourishment. From Rudolf Steiner, we can understand with this picture how destiny lived through on Earth is taken up into heaven. Both for individuals and for people in community, destiny that was transformed in the heights becomes the foundation for the destiny awaiting on Earth.

Can we stand in life in such a way that we look forward with deep longing for a destiny we can recognize? Can we look forward with an open mind to the destiny that lies before us, even though we may often lack the carefree nature of the little girl I once saw happily singing and walking in the garden? She must have been less than four years old, and she stood in the soft rain, face up, her eyes tightly closed, arms spread wide and facing upward, singing to the rain to make her grow.

The Guardian Angel

We can consciously go in search of the level of the angels. Rudolf Steiner once said:

> Just as what we have done in the past works on into our present life, the things we do in the present must work on into the future. But this is possible only through the angels, who direct their gaze to a person's present deeds and bring them to effect in the future. It is good and right to consider this function of the angels. We do many things that should bear fruit in the future. Humanity of the present age has become sadly thoughtless about such matters. When we have performed some deed, we should think of our angel, saying inwardly: *May my guardian spirit receive this, my deed, as a root, and from it bring forth fruit.* The more definite and vivid the imagery used when we address our angel in connection with deeds that should subsequently bear fruit, the more abundant this fruit can be in the future.*

* Rudolf Steiner, *Karmic Relationships*, vol. 6, p. 55 (trans. revised).

12

Incarnation in Sight

Is that a cloud bank far away on the horizon? Or is it indeed a barely visible line of land, the land to which the ship has been making its way for so long? Today, few people have any idea of what it is like to see land slowly emerging from the sea in this way. How many explorers, migrants, and, until recently, ordinary travelers looked forward to that moment with excitement. Today we seem to fall from the clouds just before landing after a period that has become increasingly short between departure and arrival.

Sometimes the picture we had imagined of the new country is immediately and drastically corrected. Shortly after the end of the Second World War, I recall being transported from the Dutch East Indies to Holland on a ship that had been used for troop transport during the war. After a voyage of five weeks, we knew that land must be near. In the final few days, the ship had been going very slowly upon a storm-tossed sea that had not yet been cleared of mines. As the boat slowed down again early one morning, this didn't seem unusual, until someone suddenly shouted, "We are there! Land!" We looked around us on that cold February morning, but there was nothing in sight, until someone pointed toward the low lines of sand dunes on both sides of the locks outside Amsterdam, which the ship had very nearly reached. It was an unexpected sight to see the land beneath our feet, especially since for most of the travelers, who had always had mountains around them in the East, this trip was not a return to their homeland but their first journey to the country their ancestors had left to go to the colonies.

We have seen that the preparation for the next incarnation, as we slowly give form to our new embodiment, actually requires the entire time between death and the coming birth. Taking a closer look at the final phase of this preparation, we will discover that, even after such a lengthy preparation, surprises might still happen.

The Spiritual Germ

During the descent from the world of spirit into the physical world, the human organism is assembled. The three higher members of our being descend from the spiritual world while the physical body is prepared within the stream of heredity from ancestors to descendants.

Together with an immense number of divine–spiritual beings, human beings live in a purely spiritual world among higher hierarchical beings. At about the middle of the time between death and the next birth, they weave the germ of the physical body. The substance of this immensely large seed is taken by the soul from the universe, having poured itself out over the cosmos. At this time we are completely absorbed with our soul—in other words, with our "I" and astral organism in the activities of the gods, in the midst of whom we live, in a way that was called intuitive in chapter 9. At the same time, we also experience that, in the planetary spheres, everything is present that we both accomplished and neglected. We know that we should not abandon that, but we also know we cannot change it; we can do this only after we return again to Earth.

Thus begins our way through the starry heavens toward Earth and to conception and birth. In the process, it seems as if those divine–spiritual beings are withdrawing. Whereas we first lived in their midst, now we experience their revelation as a reflection of their earlier presence. Because of the afterimages we observe in a sort of cosmic, inspirational consciousness, we begin to feel autonomous. An inner "I" grows in us, an individually experienced "I." With this increasing self-consciousness, as we are becoming estranged from the divine worlds, a desire grows ever stronger for embodiment; the spiritual germ begins to develop in the direction of a body, albeit a spiritual body.

Earlier we felt the cosmos in our inner being, which means that we experienced only purely divine–spiritual beings. In a next phase, we begin to experience their afterimages, which leads to our first sensation of a world outside our self. We become aware of the Sun, the fixed stars, and the planets, but this happens "from the other side"; we begin to notice planetary movements. Thus we come within reach of the spiritual Moon forces. They are the forces that gradually lead us out of the spiritual world and into physical existence. We leave the spiritual cosmos and enter the etheric cosmos, coming a step closer to the Earth.

Once the afterimages of the divine–spiritual beings have become star signs and constellations, we enter what we experience on Earth as our cosmos. In this "earthly cosmos" we sense how the spiritual germ of our physical body is calling more and more for embodiment, but it is still a spiritual body untouched by earthly existence.

Yes, even at this point, our still purely spiritual physical body is completely undifferentiated; one body looks like any other, much like grains of wheat. What we do know is that one of those bodies that look so much alike is our own. We will take possession of it on Earth, but for the time being it interests us only as an expression of the cosmic secrets among which we have lived, and it seems no different from all the other bodies.

Differentiation and Individualization

The decision to become either a woman or a man is not made until we enter the spiritual force field of the Moon. If we want to become a woman, we have to choose a time to descend to the Earth when the Full Moon is shining; if we want to become a man, it has to be New Moon. From its illuminated side, the Moon sends the forces into the universe that we need to become a man; from its dark side come the forces we need to become a woman. In these latter forces, we perceive certain beings who prepare us to become a woman.

Thus, at a certain moment in the etheric cosmos, we decide the gender in which we want to appear on Earth. But this descent does not necessarily happen very quickly. As a future man, after being exposed to the spiritual forces of the New Moon, we might also want to experience thc spiritual forces of the Full Moon. If we do this, it will show in our future head in particular—for instance, as brown eyes and black hair. If we want to become a woman but also want to experience the spiritual forces of the New Moon, we might have blue eyes and blond hair.

Similarly, we also pass through the other planetary spheres and enter their force fields. For example, if we have been prepared for it by destiny, the position of Saturn in the constellation of Leo will give us the potential of reacting intelligently to what life brings us; when meeting adversity we won't give up. Such pre-birth dispositions can be strengthened by the appropriate upbringing and education or be weakened or rendered ineffective.

We might also be together with the spiritual beings reflected in the constellation of Aries and who work on our future head. When we then move on and collaborate in Taurus with the heavenly powers living there, we work on the relationship between our larynx and lungs. If Mars now directs the light from its backside in this direction, the movement of Mars expresses everything we did right or neglected on Earth through our organs of speech. Every lie we spoke shines toward us spiritually there. Things such as this influence us as we work on this part of our speech organs. The inner planets prepare us for the family and the ethnicity in which we will appear; the sphere of Venus affects the family, and that of Mercury affects our ethnicity.

Just before we arrive at the beginning of our earthly career, the spiritual germ falls away from us; it had continued to shrink on the way down. It descends to Earth as a composite of forces and is quickly received by the stream of heredity fused by the father and mother. Thus, the spiritual processes we experienced "up there" are continued physically "down here" on Earth.

Whereas we surrender what we have woven in the cosmos, we remain behind as soul and spirit. We know that we are connected with what fell away from us on the way down, but we cannot unite with it directly. This leads to a strong sense of deprivation, and in this state of hardship we begin to gather the forces for our etheric body. We attract from the world ether what we need for our etheric organism, after which we are ready to move into a physical body on Earth.

At birth, we receive a kind of model of our physical body from our parents and ancestors. During the first seven years, we individualize this model; we make it our own with what we brought from the spiritual world. The baby teeth, for instance, are a product of heredity; we generate our permanent teeth from what we brought with us; we do the same with our whole organism, because we can no longer gather a physical body in the visible, physical world (which is carried by centripetal spiritual forces) in the same way this is still possible for the etheric body in the world of centrifugal spiritual forces.

"Original sin" (or "inherited sin") forced us to obtain our body from our ancestors on Earth. Following Rudolf Steiner, I am not using this concept as it is commonly used by theologians, to denote a kind of inevitable sinful nature that is a Calvinist counterpart of hell, used to keep people effectively under control; sinfulness to which we are supposedly subject at birth through heredity and a consequence of the Fall of the first human beings described in the Bible.* With this shadowy picture and under the spell of all sorts of fascinating, personal variations of "sinfulness," the cart was once put before the horse. I am using the concept "inherited sin" in the way that we are burdened by heredity and forced to derive our existence from our ancestors with all its consequences, rather than from the spiritual world.

Into this model, which is thus made available to us, are also imprinted all the imperfections of those who preceded us on Earth in a personal sense, and we add to those the

* Rudolf Steiner, *Karmic Relationships*, vol. 1, p. 80; the English translation there uses the words *inherited sin*—i.e., "from our ancestors."

imperfections we bring with us that we have thus far been unable to transform. It is a model that, to the extent possible, has to be adapted by us; we see how children make great efforts in this during their first seven years. It can make them seriously ill, but those who are no longer able to incur the childhood diseases risk going through life afflicted by a grey mass of non-individualized humanness. Throughout the first half of life, we make every effort to graft our destiny onto the body we were given. Parents will observe, with some emotion, inherited characteristics in their children—"just like her mother" or "exactly like his grandfather." Inherited characteristics are the result of our inner urge of wanting particular parents. It is our hope for the best opportunity to become ourselves, which is expressed especially during the second seven-year cycle in our inner, moral bond with them.

Etheric Body and Astral Organism

We gather our etheric body in the world ether after conception when we have been left behind, so to speak, by ourselves and have handed off the spiritual germ of our future body as a composite of forces. We incorporate into our etheric body the entire memory of our destiny—our destiny in its true destiny-forming forces. The etheric body then also contains an extract of the etheric body of the previous life, which was not surrendered when it was integrated into the etheric world. The essence of our previous etheric body permeates the new one as it is gathered and formed from the whole cosmos. This takes place through the Moon forces, which awake a longing in us to realize our destiny on Earth.

The angels of the third hierarchy work in the Moon forces; these angels form the character of our destiny expressed in our constitution. First we experience the revelation of the spiritual beings in their afterimages; then we experience their activity.* Through this, the will toward the Earth lights up in us, especially in our destiny. Once the etheric body connects with the astral body and "I," it can unite with the embryo and take the place of the etheric body of the mother, which then withdraws.

The astral organism contains everything that life between death and the coming birth has yielded but this never comes into our consciousness during earthly life. In intimate contact with other human and spiritual beings, all that happened in the previous life becomes reflected in it. With sympathy, higher spiritual beings can take up what has the right to exist in the universe; with antipathy, they reject what will remain part of our destiny. Thus the web of destiny awaiting us on Earth comes into being.

We work together with the people with whom we are connected because of our spiritual physiognomy, especially during the middle of our time together in the spiritual world. We see our self in them, reflected in our deeds, and this gives us our feeling as an "I"-being. However, in the spiritual world this is not an experience within ourselves, but a reflection from our

---

* "Divine Spirit is expressed in the cosmos in various ways and in successive stages: first, through its own inmost being; second, through manifestation of that being; third, through activity when its being withdraws from manifestation; and fourth, through the finished work, when the Divine is no longer present in the outwardly visible universe, but only Divine forms" (Carl Unger, *Language of the Consciousness Soul: A Guide to Rudolf Steiner's "Leading Thoughts,"* p. 186). Later, Steiner referred to these four phases in descriptions of the human being's descent to Earth. Doing so, we follow the ways that the divine–spiritual beings also went. See, for example, Steiner, *The Inner Nature of Man,* lect. 6.

surroundings. We can recognize ourselves in the nature of our destiny in all the effects of our deeds that were thus reflected back to us. These reflections concentrate at a certain time during the last third of our time in the spiritual world and form our astral body. We enter life with this disposition.

The astral body formed in the spiritual world also connects our "destiny package" (which we have come to know as the second human with our "moral values") that we had to leave behind in the Moon sphere after our previous life. In the past, before Christ appeared on Earth, the lofty spiritual being of the Sun helped humans take up this second human being into themselves even before birth so that destiny would live in the soul and not lodge itself in the body; otherwise, bodies would have been born that were not viable or were afflicted by diseases. Ever since then, at the beginning of the ascent and toward the end of the descent, Christ (whom we can now meet on Earth) gives us the strength to handle this moral human being. We receive the strength to accept our destiny in freedom and to take on the consequences of our deeds. We have become free human beings through this loving help of Christ.

There is another reason why Christ's help is important at the end of the descent to earthly life. When we are in the sphere of the Moon, we meet the group souls of the animals in their continuously changing harmony and disharmony, a kind of surging up and down like clouds of mist; the moral human being we left behind in the Moon sphere also lives in the midst of them. We have to keep this wild activity away from us as much as possible so that we do not become overwhelmed by all sorts of passions and instincts in the coming life. Thanks to a true religious, selfless disposition, we receive the forces we need for this through the mediation of Christ.

At conception, when the spiritual germ is integrated in the embryo that begins to grow in the mother's body, we are left to ourselves in the sphere of the Moon, as we have seen. Our feeling of privation there causes us to begin the formation of our new etheric body. Consequently, the soul can connect itself, along with the etheric body, with the manifesting embryo. Thus we bring our destiny to the Earth, and not until this point does our physical body receive an individual form.

All spiritual germs that take possession of physical germs at conception are completely alike. In the world of spirit, we weave *the* spiritual germ of the earthly body like everyone else. The coming physical body becomes *our* body only because of the destiny that, through the etheric body, connects with the physical germ. This happens in the third week after conception.

"I" and "I"-Organization

As long as possible, the spiritual germ preserves the spherical form that enabled it to exist in the spiritual world in the spiritual domain of the globe. During the ascent, we assumed the form of the Sun and laid the spiritual foundation for our future upper pole. On the way back, in Mars existence, the spiritual germ is laid for the rhythmic and metabolic–limb systems added to the upper pole. When we go through the Sun sphere again during the descent, our moral being comes together; it begins to beat in the seminal form of the heart that is added there. Then our gaze is directed downward toward the ancestors who will lead us to our future parents. In Sun existence, we also receive the spiritual basis of our limb system; the Moon, Mercury, and Venus, so to speak, become our limbs, which will be formed primarily in typical earthly forms present in the area of the Earth where our ancestors and parents are mainly living.

The system of forces we call the "I"-organization comes into being with the inner "I" during the descent, when the soul begins to move among the afterimages of the spiritual beings in whose midst it dwelled before. At this stage, it is still wholly a reflection, an image filled with forces. The "I"-organization creates the spiritual pattern that will structurally permeate the physical body once it can enter that body through the mediation of the etheric body. After the birth, through the astral, etheric, and physical bodies, it will help the growth of the lower pole and come to expression in everything that is the inner power of movement. It will more directly help the upper pole through the nerves.

Now we see a process that does not build up but destroys when the spirit intervenes directly in physical matter. In the lower pole, the "I" is able to work only after having permeated itself with the soul forces of the astral organism. Then the "I" takes the astral and etheric forces into itself and flows upward in the blood, in a building process that regenerates the human being.

Long before conception, we have already set our sights on specific ancestors and specific parents, sometimes when those people are still on their own way to birth. In doing so, we are aware of spiritual realities and intentions that literally have to wait for centuries before they can come to realization. As we are preparing for our birth, before conception we receive a picture of what the physical situation on Earth is like, at first mainly through our future mother.* We look down toward her especially. We receive an idea of our future father through the image of him that our mother has in her soul. However, if our father is to play an important role in the heredity we need to receive, for

* Rudolf Steiner, *Artistic Sensitivity as a Spiritual Approach to Knowing Life and the World*, p. 54.

example, we can also have a direct picture of him. In this case, the picture we will have of our mother becomes less distinct.

But our mother will always bring the basis of the physical body and etheric body. Everything that comes to us in the spiritual, archetypal form of the head connects itself with this from our sojourn in the world of spirit. Through fertilization, the "I" and astral body connect with those two bodies. The lower pole is built from the Earth after the fertilization, and the typical earthly form of the place on Earth where we are headed works in it.

We are dependent on the heredity from our parents only in the middle region of heart and lungs. Once we are human beings on Earth, through our head we can experience ourselves as citizens of suprasensory spheres; in the heart and lung systems, we can find a relationship from human being to human being; and through the metabolic system, we belong to the Earth of which we are a part.

But it is the astral body, formed as described above, that looks for the motherly part of the two parents. The "I" pulls us toward the fatherly part. If the astral body and "I" are drawn toward two people who have no connection, the "I" continues to search until a fitting pair is found. Thus it should not be a surprise that, in addition to the half-dreaming, half-prophetic impressions that expecting mothers have of their child, there are fathers who also receive such impressions.

The freedom to accept our destiny as described here has had an unexpected consequence ever since Archangel Michael, the countenance of Christ, made the destiny of human beings his direct concern in the late nineteenth century. In the future, when human beings have taken on their destiny and connected it with the etheric body, they can make a far-reaching decision before they definitively take possession of their physical body.

In this connection of destiny with the etheric body, we see our destiny in all its details before us, and we can see how much we have injured others in our previous lives. In the light Michael shines on this insight and borne by the love of Christ, human beings can decide to entrust to someone else the body they had prepared for themselves and then assume the body that the other human being had prepared for rebirth. This means that, in the future, acceptance of destiny will have concrete significance.

We have seen that in our future destiny the coming incarnation begins to become a reality first around the middle of the period we spend in the world of spirit. It happens during the ascent when the astral body has separated and the soul lives on in the "I." We have the overwhelming experience of knowing that we are still within this body of the stars, yet feel freed from it. When this body (which we know is our body of destiny) fades into the far distances, we also lose the connection with ourselves, the one we have become through all our previous incarnations. In the cosmic midnight hour, however, we find ourselves again; we see ourselves coming back from oblivion into our future destiny, surrounded by those with whom we are related in some way.

Destiny is human beings first and foremost; it is the web that connects us to others with whom we must accomplish something, whether old or new relationships.

The future homeland that emerges is also human beings; it is the joint future of those who are connected with one another. It becomes concrete in the ancestors toward whom we look when we are in the Sun sphere, the spiritual heart of the world. It receives form in the human communities with which we want to connect ourselves. Destiny is created when we are embedded in the realm of the protective spiritual beings who help us between death and a new birth to overcome the temptation to remain in the spiritual world; they help us to remain true to ourselves. Destiny is also created through the fulfillment of unfinished affairs, fulfilling the consequences of having been embodied on Earth.

From Life to Life with Meditative Verses

Now that we have reached the end of our exploration of all that we go through before birth, several meditative verses by Rudolf Steiner follow. We see those who are our destiny appear to us through these meditative verses. The first is addressed to a soul who has just concluded an earthy life and is having difficulties adapting to its new mode of existence:

> May my love be the sheaths
> that now surround you,
> cooling your warmth,
> warming your cold.
> interwoven through sacrifice,
> live carried upward by love,
> gifted with light.*

The next two verses reflect the situation of the soul in the spiritual world:

> May our love follow you
> O soul, living there in spirit,
> seeing your earthly life,
> beholding yourself cognized as spirit.
> And what in the land of souls
> in thinking appears to you
> to be yourself—
> receive our love

* Rudolf Steiner, *Our Dead*, p. 331.

so that we may feel ourselves in you
and you may find in our souls
what lives with you in faithfulness.*

In the shining ones
I feel
the power of life.
Death has awakened me
from sleep,
from spiritual sleep.
Out of myself
I will become and do
what the power of light
streams into me.**

The next verse is about the human being between death and the next birth. It grew from Steiner's descriptions in one of his lectures on karma, given on July 4, 1924. He used the names of the nine angelic realms (outlined in chapter 6):

Angels, Archangels, and Archai
in the ether weaving
receive the human being's
web of destiny.
In Exousiai, Dynamis, and Kyriotetes,
in the astral feeling of the cosmos
the righteous consequences
of the earthly human life
die into the realm of being.
In Thrones and Cherubim and Seraphim,
as their deeds of being,
the justly transmuted fruits
of the earthly human life
are resurrected.***

---

* Ibid., p. 334.
** Ibid.
*** Rudolf Steiner, *Karmic Relationships*, vol. 3, p. 36.

With the final verse, we are standing at the cradle of a small sleeping child, and we address ourselves with all our warmth and love to this human being who began a new incarnation so recently:

> May light stream into you that can take hold of you;
> I follow its rays with the warmth of my love.
> I think with my thinking's best thoughts of joy
> on the stirring of your heart.
> Thoughts to strengthen you,
> thoughts to carry you,
> thoughts to cleanse you.
> I want to gather my thoughts of joy
> before the steps of your life,
> that they bind themselves to your will for life,
> so that it finds itself with strength
> in all the world,
> evermore,
> through itself.*

Helpful beings have assisted us though all times, both in the world of spirit and now on Earth, so that, as it is expressed here, our will for life will find itself in strength, everywhere and evermore, through itself.

* Rudolf Steiner, *Prayers for Parents and Children*, p. 7.

13

Conclusion: The Human Being — a Risky Venture

"The human being really comes into the world as a mirror image," Rudolf Steiner said in one of his best-known lectures about pre-birth life.* We are asked to consolidate this reflection, to prove it true in our development between birth and death. In that lecture, Steiner described how conception reflects an event in the spiritual world, a cosmic world process that takes place between the Sun and Earth. The feminine element at conception is influenced by the Sun, the masculine by the Earth. This happens when we are about to be born and have already had the vision of how things will be on Earth.

Whereas conception is a reflection of this process between Sun and Earth, which takes place in the parents, the subsequent life of the embryo reflects an earlier phase of the pre-birth process, between what is left from pre-earthly Ancient Moon and pre-earthly Ancient Sun.** We find a remnant of this process in the ten lunar months of pregnancy; it recalls the cosmic period of Ancient Moon.

The third reflection follows during the first years of childhood, the period when a child begins to babble and is still without

---

* Rudolf Steiner, *Artistic Sensitivity as a Spiritual Approach to Knowing Life and the World*, p. 54.

** See appendix 3; also, Rudolf Steiner, *An Outline of Esoteric Science*, chap. 4, "Cosmic Evolution and the Human Being.

a clear idea of the self. Those first years reflect the forces that work between the planets and the Sun; they recall the period of Ancient Sun. During those years, the forces present in infants strive outward; it is our task to facilitate the mirror image of this phase of the pre-birth process to become reality in the child. We create the right spiritual climate for this with thoughts and feelings expressed in the prayer that begins, "May light stream into you."

The fourth and last reflection of the pre-birth process tends to consolidate itself in the whole subsequent period of childhood, when a person can still be brought up by others. What strives outward in this period are the forces that, in an even earlier phase of life between death and rebirth, worked between the stars in the heavens and the planets. They are processes that recall the cosmic period of pre-earthly Ancient Saturn. After that, the time has passed when we can be brought up by others. Then we are sent into the world as free human beings, and the only processes that are still reflected belong to the period that precedes Ancient Saturn; they do not belong to the visible world.

We clearly recognize in this description the phases of the soul's descent as summarized at the beginning of the previous chapter. It is noteworthy that, in the first phase, the female side of the parents is influenced by the Sun, whereas in the subsequent pregnancy the mother will follow the rhythm of the Moon. We realize, too, that becoming a human being continues to reflect the phases of a process of incarnation that we once went through together with our planet Earth.

Later in 1915, Rudolf Steiner mentioned in passing another instance of mirroring. What happens to us right after death could be compared to what the physical body goes through after birth.* The life panorama that constitutes the world of the deceased during the first days after death also prepares itself to become a living cosmos. Subsequently, when this most personal inner cosmos becomes clothed in streams of light and sound, the etheric body can separate and integrate into the etheric world. Similarly, we are clothed in human substance at birth, in which the soul experiences its connection to the Earth.

We have already become acquainted with the process whereby the soul adapts to the world it enters at death or birth by gradually adopting the form appropriate for the new way of existence. After death, the soul gradually assumes the spherical form of a globe; when we prepare for birth, we adopt in our lower pole the forms that are specifically appropriate for the Earth.

Processes in Reflection

At birth, as well as when we die, we witness processes that reflect each other in several respects. In our first human developments when we come into the world, we mirror events that occur when we leave the world of spirit. In the transition from the one world to the other, the phases of adaptation, during which we familiarize ourselves with that other world, are also reflections of each other. Just before birth and just before dying, something needs to happen whereby these reflections are called into being. This is the moment of being "turned inside out," when we become invisible after death and physically perceptible before birth. This is how the transition is made between visibility and invisibility, between a spiritual outer world and a spiritual inner world.

---

* Rudolf Steiner, *Die geistigen Hintergründen des Ersten Weltkrieges* (The Spiritual background of World War I: Cosmic and human history, vol. 7.), Nov. 23, 1915.

However, there is yet another reflection. In our life after death, experiences during the second sojourn in the Sun sphere on our descent after the midnight hour reflect those we gain in the first sojourn there during the ascent. At the end of the ascent, we have an experience of total abandonment and loneliness, an experience of a soul in spiritual darkness with only a vague idea of a spiritual outer world. Then, in forceful inner activity, the about-face comes that connects us with our past on Earth. In this experience, we are the acting entity ourselves, the "author" that, as expressed by Benjamin Franklin, begins to prepare a "new edition" of ourself and, doing so, calls the moment of reflecting into being.

With the aid of these two moments of reflection, in our minds we can picture the journey from life to death and into the next life. One moment takes place close to earthly embodiment, the other deep in the world of spirit. The image of an ellipse might arise in us with two focal points that determine its shape. We have come to know both reflections, far away and nearby, as processes and developments in phases. They are partly physiognomic in nature; for instance, when in the transition to a different mode of existence, we have to adapt our form to the new situation. Developments related to the experience of the midnight hour have to do with the transformation of soul forces and have a purely inner nature; however, we have to realize that this is an inwardness in which inner is simultaneously outer.

In such reflections, we are dealing at the same time with both object and image. However, in the course of incarnation, the actual process takes place before birth and the reflection after. With processes in the spiritual world, the reflection consists of the fact that we go through the phases of a process in reverse. This occurs prior to birth and after death, as well as in the midnight hour, the other focal point of our life.

It is always difficult, however, to handle concepts such as mirroring, reflection, and reality. Plato was still able to picture the connection between reality and reflection in the image of the cave with the fire at the entrance, in front of which figures moved and cast shadows on the back wall. In our current way of thinking, it is usually considered strange to say that what we have visibly before us is not the whole reality. This is a good point to reflect on the way Rudolf Steiner handled the concept of reality.

Reality Can Be Found Only in Context

Rudolf Steiner once pointed out that a rose in a vase is only an apparent reality.* The flower cannot actually exist without the rose bush that roots in the earth. Similarly, our finger is no longer part of our organism if it is severed from the hand. When we deal with reality in our usual casual way, we face isolated phenomena to which we attribute abstract associations. In many of the sciences—geology and biology, for instance—we first remove phenomena from their context and then treat them as though they exist in a kind of vacuum. Then we give them a place in an abstraction of reality.

However, we are dealing with reality only within a context, such as that of a rose on the rose bush or the finger on the hand. The Earth that geologists study, like a rose in a vase or a severed finger, is merely an apparent and temporary reality. The Earth is not real without the human being; the human being is not reality without the Earth. It is a form of materialism

* Rudolf Steiner, *Understanding Society through Spiritual–Scientific Knowledge*, Nov. 9, 1919.

to think that when we isolate Earth and humanity from each other we are dealing with something real.

The fact that we are not real as human beings without the Earth is a fundamental experience of the soul on its path between death and a subsequent birth. Immediately after death we experience the world we left behind as incomplete without us and that we are a building stone of the world. However, the idea that Earth is not a reality without human beings is far removed from our usual way of thinking. We need Rudolf Steiner's Anthroposophy to gradually develop a feeling for the fact that humanity is an inseparable part of the organism called Earth, that we human beings are an integral part of Earth as a reality. Steiner tried to illustrate this with an experience we can have in the vicinity of Naples, Italy.* When a piece of paper is burned just above the ground, the soil begins to "smoke." Vapors rise as the air moves upward because of the burning paper and decreased air pressure, which frees the vapors. More burning paper leads to more vapors.

Now imagine the masses of people on Earth in the liveliest way possible. The billions of people have a comparable effect on the Earth in all their activities. We don't exactly see vapors rising as people move about and engage in activities, but we do have to look within the human organism for a great part of the causes of what happens in the kingdoms of nature. Forces that work on Earth and that we come to know through physics, chemistry, and mechanics are intimately related to the willpower concentrated in humans, which we normally notice only in the metabolism. Today, our will forces are closely connected with the decomposing, destructive forces at work on our planet. In fact, without a hotbed of destruction in our inmost being we

* Ibid.

would be unable to live on the Earth. However, we would be exclusively destructive if we were not in communication with the constructive forces of Earth during sleep.

Being Human on Earth

It is astonishing to realize that everything we see around us on Earth depends fundamentally on us human beings. Because of our existence here, we are jointly responsible for the Earth as it exists and develops. This realization adds another dimension to our relationship with the kingdoms of nature (chapter 11) in connection with the realization of our destiny on Earth. To a certain extent, we are the ones who appear in those realms; we recognize ourselves in our cosmic past through what comes to meet us in the kingdoms of nature. What takes place in water, earth, and air, what shines down on us from the stars, what the wind brings us—all of this has an intimate connection with us.

The extremely personal connection between humans and the realms of nature is the subject of "The Washing of the Feet" by Christian Morgenstern:

> I thank you, strong and silent stone,
> inclining gratefully before you
> to plant life with your help I've grown.
>
> I thank you, plants and Mother Earth,
> and bend in gratitude before you.
> You helped the beast in me to birth.
>
> I thank you, stone and beast and tree,
> and bow in gratitude before you.
> You helped me find my Self in me.
>
> I thank you, human being, too,
> and humbly do fall down before you,
> for we exist because you grew.

In thanks joins God upon His throne,
and all the spirits that adore Him.
In thanks all beings are at one.*

Gradually the insight may grow in us how much we owe to the beings that appear in the kingdoms of nature. When we consciously seek a relationship with the realms of nature, we begin to realize that we are actually witnessing something embryonic. Throughout our last period between death and new birth we develop the constant feeling that beings are missing from our surroundings, as if they were elsewhere in exile. Once we return to the Earth, we find those missing beings in the kingdoms of minerals and plants, although embalmed or shriveled, as it were. Animals, with their group souls that dwell in the spiritual world and bodies that lack individuality, give the impression of not belonging here. Humans and animals share a form that still has to grow after death.

Thus something begins to arise in us, about which the apostle Paul wrote in his letter to the Romans (Rom. 8:18–23). The beings that appear in the kingdoms of nature have to wait "for the children of God to be revealed," so that the forces of the future human being, "the Son of Man," can unfold. All of creation waits with great longing for this, says Paul. Creation was subjected to fruitlessness but lives in the hope of being liberated from its transience. Then it will experience the freedom of all who live as children of God in the light. Creation still suffers and sighs in its entirety, in the pangs of a new birth looking toward the radiating light of the children of God.

We recognize in these children of God those who have become able to realize the full potential of the Son of Man—those who, because of their connection with the Godhead,

* Christian Morgenstern, *We Have Found a Path.*

are able to represent their own complete reality. Through our connection with the beings that live in the other kingdoms of nature, as the community of human beings, we become truly grounded in the Earth, where we live and work. What we experience in the outer realms, still outside ourselves, is taken up into the human realm after death.

After all this it should not surprise us that, for Rudolf Steiner, insight and knowledge are not absolute. Insights are not valid for eternity, but for only a limited time, and sometimes for only a limited area of the Earth. Daily life often reminds us that an insight that is true for America, for example, might not have much significance in Asia. This explains why Steiner reacted with revulsion when, one year after the cease-fire that ended World War I, he read that one of the generals who had sent millions of men to their death calmly declared that if he were placed in the same situation again, he would make the same decisions.* This was Hindenburg, under whose presidency Adolf Hitler began his reign, and who later continued to play a role in German politics.

We need to learn from the facts we have created, said Steiner. He also said that he would never give the Goetheanum building the same form if he ever had to make a new design. When the first Goetheanum was destroyed by fire on New Year's Eve 1922, he did indeed design a completely different second Goetheanum.

Our Cosmic Task

Between death and the next birth we continuously have the sense that, as human beings, we are only partially real in the world of spirit. We sense that we need the Earth to make

* Hindenburg: see Rudolf Steiner *Understanding Society through Spiritual-Scientific Knowledge*, Nov. 14, 1919.

progress. On Earth, we seem incomplete after the archetype of our own coming existence was cast in an untimely way into space; after having gained experiences on Earth we need to continue growing after we die. Through our cycles of births we try to let the reality of the Son of Man grow into the reality of a Child of God. Only in this way can we own the forces that turn our temporary reality into true reality. Only in this way do we become an actual part of the true reality, in which the sensory and suprasensory come together. During our life on Earth, in our organism we reflect both realities of which we temporarily form part, with the heavenly reality in our upper pole and the earthly reality in our lower pole. After death we have to legitimize our earthly experiences in the spiritual world, and we receive the opportunity to practice our own reality, so to speak, in the rhythm of breathing in and breathing out spiritual social life and inner solitude.

Between birth and death, we are the reflection of what we go through in the suprasensory before our birth—a spiritual process is hidden in us, just as in every natural process. In this sense, as human beings we *are* the "process," always the temporary result of both temporary realities. During life we are only "half human," but seeming real; for we are embedded in suprasensory experiences that elude normal consciousness. We even have to gain our experiences in two fundamentally different worlds that meet in us with both centripetal and centrifugal spiritual forces.

Despite the fact that we are only "half human," seemingly real, during life on Earth, we contribute to an eventual joining of those two worlds. The Earth would contain nothing but earthly substances if human beings did not leave their physical body behind when they die. The human form, which we have spiritually and psychically imprinted into our body during life, becomes after burial or cremation part of the Earth and continues to work into its suprasensory structure. In a spiritual sense, the dead body works to refresh the Earth and to ensure that it remains inhabitable for human beings. If this did not happen continually in this hardening world, various rigidifying and petrifying tendencies would have made human incarnations impossible long ago.

However, the process through which human soul and spirit forces are communicated to our earthly environment in a particular form is not limited to our existence after death. The way we arrive in the spiritual world depends on whether we are old or young when we die. If we die young, we still have a good deal of forces in us from pre-birth. We make an intimate connection between the forces we bring with us and the experiences we gain in the physical world. After dying, we bring this into the world of spirit, which we share with other human beings, and give it a certain weight that it would otherwise not have.

Alternatively, if we have grown to an advanced age, the connection between what we brought with us into earthly life and our experiences in life has loosened and the reverse happens after death. From a certain age, said Rudolf Steiner, we unite our own being, drop by drop, as it were, with what is spiritually present on Earth.* Having grown old and while "squeezing out" spiritual substance, we make the physical Earth more spiritual than it would otherwise be. In our advanced age we bring spiritual substance into the physical Earth, whereas those who die young take physical substance into the spiritual world.

* Rudolf Steiner, *Human Evolution: A Spiritual–Scientific Quest*, Sept. 2, 1918.

Creating Balance in Freedom

Rudolf Steiner placed the cosmic task of human beings (aspects of which have been mentioned) in the larger context of the activities of Lucifer and Ahriman, the two spiritual powers who each wish to create their own exclusive world. Both are indispensable in the cosmos, although for humankind they are often called necessary evil. We can view them as the two sides of a scale, which can get out of balance in, for example, the direction of flight into spirit or hardening into matter. It is then the task of human beings to function as the "balance beam," all the while maintaining equilibrium between the two extremes to deny them the opportunity to persist in their exclusive one-sidedness (see appendix 6).

In our present circumstances, human beings cannot avoid the activities of the centripetal spiritual powers and their rigidifying world. If we did not die a little each day, we would not possess consciousness. What we are able to generate in the way of conscious spiritual presence on Earth we owe to the continuous dying process in our body. What we bring after death into the spiritual world from the Earth must not only undergo a complete metamorphosis, but in our spiritual form what used to be our head even gradually fades away.

Death, which followed the Fall into sin, has had profound effects in the creation that was called into being "in the beginning." The creative Godhead, which the first chapter of Genesis knows as the unity of the seven Elohim, created our world and then the human being. The Elohim, also known as the Exousiai or spirits of form, have always been the creative spirits in the inner essence of the human being up to our time. Now, however, the Archai are beginning to be creatively active in human nature. They went through their human stage at the beginning of the parallel path of human and cosmic evolution. Having risen in the realms of the angels, they are beginning to assume the creative work of the Exousiai. Thus, we human beings will increasingly have opportunities to realize the need to be free; we will be able to respond to the revealing activity of the Archai in freedom through our own activity.

It is in our head, which is based only on a reflection of the spiritual primordial form, that as human beings we can feel ourselves free and are able to think thoughts that are themselves reflections. This is where the creative activity of the Archai starts. It counts on our activity as human beings, those who, thanks to a focused development of their spiritual consciousness, can "come into conversation" with these angels.

We prepare this conversation with them as we learn to live with visual representations and imaginations. In this way we create the conditions for a conversation based on mutual exchange, a conversation such as we are used to having with other people. This is one more stimulant to develop an individual spiritual life of our own in a physical body that is slowly becoming fragile.

New possibilities—new challenges! We can familiarize ourselves with the fact that we humans, no matter how you look at it, form part of a developing cosmos. We can gradually penetrate the spiritual realities behind the scenes of our visible world. We can decide for ourselves to be an active part of it and to accept the challenge of the Spirits of the Beginning, also called the Spirits of Personality.

Working Consciously with Sleeping and Waking

It is our task as human beings not only to create balance between two extremes that each strive for exclusivity. Again and again, two diametrically opposed worlds come into contact with each other through us, worlds of centripetal and centrifugal spiritual forces. When we sleep, our everyday "I" and astral body enter the realm of the centripetal beings. They communicate during sleep with the true "I" and astral body, of which they are mirror images, always dwelling in the *other* spiritual world. Knowing this, we cannot expect sleep to be merely a time of rest after being awake. Viewed from this perspective, there are actually only two moments of rest—the moment of falling asleep and the moment of waking up.

What is sleep, then, if it is not rest? It is the opposite of being awake in the way that debts are the opposite of assets. It is the condition we all know through our own dreams, in which our bodily constitution is somewhat reflected and nothing obeys the laws of space and time. In this condition, the true "I" unfolds in service to the formation of destiny, which at that point still takes place as pictures as it goes back successively through the experiences of our day, our life, and our prior lives.

In the moments of rest between our activities of being awake and sleeping we go through a kind of zero point; these two moments share a clear relationship to each other. When we try to imagine in a movement what we go through in the alternation of being awake and sleeping in twenty-four hours we come to a line in the form of a lemniscate. The two points of rest coincide in one point, and we realize that the outside of the one loop forms the inside of the other; outer becomes inner, then inner becomes outer. In the progression of our life, in the constant alternation of being awake and sleeping, we can see this form in natural movement. We do not find a "stack" of lemniscates that cover each other, but a spiraling movement of successive lemniscates.

In sleep, the "I" and astral body hand over the experiences gained during being awake to their own realities. In communicating with them, they come into contact with the spiritual powers in whose world they are dwelling. Those powers take up what can exist in their world and have to reject what can exist only somewhere else. In this confrontation, the "I," which is of the nature of all will, develops distinct forms according to its moral nature; it shrivels up because of the evil it brings with it, and it unfolds freely in the good it carries. We witness a preview, as it were, of the experiences in kamaloka described in chapters 2 and 11. Even in sleep, the "I" therefore develops moral content. The astral body is absorbed in its own world, which has more the nature of the soul.

Whereas forms are imprinted on the "I," the astral body takes on the "tint" of the feelings it bears in it—a tint that we can imagine like a color, a sound, or even a taste. The "I" and the astral body have their connection with our lower pole in shape and tone. But here, the forms of a human head are already appearing first as a reflection. Indeed, this is how, when we sleep, our future person begins to emerge in the moral forms and shades of our everyday experiences—that is, the person who, after death, becomes physiognomy in the world of spirit.

Putting One's House in Order

Our moral being thus appears in all its variations during sleep, meaning that we actually direct an unspoken question to the spiritual powers we meet in sleep—the question of our moral nature. Their answer appears in the growing forms of the "I" and the hues of the astral body; when we awake, this answer works unconsciously in us as the voice of conscience and as our inner moral disposition. No one with any life experience will want to ignore Paul's advice: "Do not let the sun go down upon your wrath" (Eph. 4:26). What we offer as question and what we receive as answer will be different if we have put our house in order within ourselves before we fall asleep. A conscious review of the events and experiences of the day leads to a "digestion" process through which the nature of our questions will change.

We might gradually develop a feeling for what Rudolf Steiner called the "holiness of sleep" if we recognize that sleep unites us with the spiritual world; it sends us up into the spiritual world. We can end our review of the day with these words: *"I am going to sleep; until I wake, my soul will be in the spiritual world. There it will meet the guiding power of my earthly life who hovers around my head; there it will meet my genius. And when I awake, I shall have had the meeting with my genius. The wings of my genius will have come into contact with my soul."** Thus we prepare for our meeting with the divine powers to whom we offer our morality each night through the intermediary of our angel.

We would all fail in the risky venture of being human if we did not learn, to some small extent at least, to draw our most important impulses from the spiritual world. Our own personal connection with the spiritual world, therefore, has to become as concrete as we can possibly make it. Only then do we become part of a living, cohesive whole that is completely real in the sense described at the beginning of this chapter.

Preparing for the Day

About two years after Rudolf Steiner spoke about the holiness of sleep, he pointed out that we unconsciously preview

* Rudolf Steiner, *Building Stones for an Understanding of the Mystery of Golgotha*, p. 45.

at night what we will experience the next day. The one who consciously experiences this with us is our angel. When we preview the coming day with that being, we negotiate, one could say, what we will do that day; we can then take thoughts and even decisions into the day. Eventually, we will notice that we cannot make the right decisions unless we awake with them in the morning, and if we are forced to make decisions based on something that happens during the day it is best to sleep on them first. For this reason the moment of waking up must also be sacred for us:

> The moment of waking should be holy for modern humanity. We should feel: I come from the spiritual world and enter the physical. All that is good, all that makes me capable of being a reasonable person, I experienced between going to sleep and waking up through conversation with the spiritual world, through conversation with those who have died and whom I knew in life and who died before me—in other words, through conversation with those who are no longer in a physical body. I experience it when I am with them in the purely spiritual world. From this experience I should develop a basic mood of holy regard for the moment of waking; this fundamental feeling will then make it possible throughout the day for me to say in one instance, "Here I am helped by a spiritual impulse," and in another, "Here I receive no help; this must not be decided before tomorrow."*

Our Future Homeland Is Human Beings

We can make yet another kind of review by looking less at the events that gave form to our life and more at the people

---

* Rudolf Steiner, *Problems of Society: An Esoteric View, from Luciferic Past to Ahrimanic Future*, June 12, 1919.

who have been involved in it, those who have been important to us and have meant something to us in life, such as parents, siblings, relatives, friends, classmates, teachers, and colleagues at work. Thus we don't so much look at what happened in and to us, but try to form a valid and distinct image of the people who surrounded us in life. We might even become overwhelmed by all the many things we have received from them. What is left as our own input compared to all they have meant to us, including all those we might have lost track of or might have died long ago? The feelings that then arise in us might grow into real self-knowledge.

If we always try to view others who have helped us become who we now are in this way, we will gradually be able to meet another person in such a way that we can see through their "packaging" as the image of their true being arises in us. We will also glimpse the activity of divine powers in them.

As we saw in the introduction, to meet another person, we take turns allowing the other to doze off a little. Only those who are on the way to their next birth have direct, conscious connections with others and with the divine powers concerned with them and their destiny. If we learn to look back as described at those who have played a role in our life, we prepare our self to play an active role in a developing cosmos, both in the future afterlife that opens up for us after death and on Earth, which is not complete without us, as we learn in life between death and a new birth.

Our future homeland is human beings—people together on this Earth, regardless of the cosmic form it might develop in the future. This means we have to connect with the work in angelic realms. This is the only way we can reach the degree of reality needed to consolidate our relationship with the Earth.

Moreover, it means that, in the future, it will become an actual defect in our soul constitution if we cannot see in others how what lives in their soul has come from a prior life.

We have to become accustomed to understanding life between birth and death in all its aspects and consequences as a continuation of the life we led prior to birth. This means we have to start paying attention to the cracks and openings that have grown during the past few decades in the soul's curtain separating us from the world of spirit. These develop because, in Steiner's words, we are crossing the threshold of the spiritual world without noticing it.* In an astonishing way, part of our existence after death is already becoming a concrete reality during our present life, including our life with the dead and with the spiritual powers, with whose help we prepare for our next life.

---

* Rudolf Steiner, *The Problems of Our Time*, Sept. 12, 1919. p. 30.

Appendices

Journeys beyond the Text

Appendix 1: The Form Body and the Body of Formative Forces

(*See the Introduction*)

Just as in my book *What Happens after We Die?* I have used the term *form body* again in this book for the suprasensory aspect of the physical body. This might lead to problems because the term is very similar to *body of formative forces*, a term that is used to indicate the etheric body, or life body. To avoid misunderstandings, I want to discuss the "form body" in reference to the spiritual physical body, the body in which forming forces are solidified.

I have found only one place where Steiner dealt extensively with this form body—namely, in a series of lectures in October 1911.* He described it as something that gives form to our body, the form principle of our appearance. It is "the idea" of our body, a concrete but invisible figure that holds the material substance together, a body of forces so transparent that it is invisible; it is our original "physical body."

In the course of human history on Earth, this transparent, original figure of our body became clouded, obscured, and filled with physical matter, so to speak. Thus our current physical body manifested in what the Bible describes as the Fall into sin. The consequence is that we return to dust at the end of our life, "for dust you are and to dust you will return" (Gen. 3:19). Through his resurrection, Christ healed and restored this

---

* Rudolf Steiner, *From Jesus to Christ*, Oct. 10, 11, 12, 1911.

original non-material figure in his resurrection body. Paul was the first to recognize this clearly.

In the lectures mentioned, Steiner used the word *phantom* for this form body. This happened soon after he had been speaking to people who were accustomed to theosophic terminology. It seems the word can be easily misunderstood because it suggests ghosts and apparitions, and because we use the word *phantom pain* in the case of pain in body parts that are no longer there.

"Form Body" and "Body of Formative Forces"

We might ask: What is the difference between the spiritual form of the physical body filled with forces (the *form body*) and the etheric body, for which Rudolf Steiner used the term *body of formative forces*.

First, there is the difference of age. What we call the physical body is actually a fourfold whole with a fourfold cosmic past. After its beginning during the cosmic phase of Ancient Saturn, it changed in the subsequent phase of Ancient Sun, when the etheric body was added to it. It evolved to receive the young astral body during the phase of Ancient Moon and the "I"-organization at the beginning of our own Earth period. We have all of this in us, but only the earthly aspect of it is visible; the other parts are invisible.

These parts all consist of composites of streams, which in turn consist of forces that work on and into each other. Our threefold invisible body is made visible through food intake and blood circulation. At conception, as a spiritual germ, these composites connect with the earthly seed to form the fourfold physical body. Therefore, nothing physical will remain if we imagine the absence of everything that is filled by food. What remains is a suprasensory composite of forces, the human form. Our physical body goes back to this original invisible, suprasensory form that shapes and maintains the human figure.

Viewed cosmically, the etheric body is younger than the physical body. It came into being during the evolutionary phase of Ancient Sun; thus it is always behind the physical body in its development. It is less perfected than the physical body, though it enables the physical body to live. We might view it as a kind of architect of the physical body. By permeating it, the streams and forces of the etheric body maintain our organs in their form and structure.

The intimate connection between the etheric body and everything that has been "Sun" on Earth is also apparent after death. The deceased seek their way toward the world of spirit through the East, toward the rising Sun. We have to draw from our existence in the Sun sphere between death and the next birth the forces needed to obtain our etheric body again in the right way before birth.

More could be said about the age of the physical body and the etheric body. We witness how our physical body ages; we gradually get wrinkles, and we become weaker and have ailments. The etheric body grows in the opposite direction; it begins "old" and completely formed and becomes younger as it loses its finely chiseled form and becomes fresh again. It becomes cosmic again after having been completely absorbed into the physical body during the growth of this body. Those who are able to see it witness an image of outer creative force, just as during childhood the physical body is the expression of an outer, rosy, creative force. When we die the etheric body is truly young.

Appendix 2: The Resurrection Body

(See chapter 1)

St. Paul was the first to see clearly that the body in which the resurrected Christ appeared was a completely renewed body. He saw that Christ in the resurrection body restored the original nonmaterial form of the human being.

Paul did not meet Christ as Jesus the human being who was still grappling with the consequences of the Fall. At Damascus, the resurrected Lord appeared in his resurrection body to Paul, dazzling in a light brighter than the Sun. Paul describes in his first letter to the Corinthians what he discovered later during his three-year sojourn in the Arabian desert (1 Cor. 15).

In our human body on Earth, Paul realized that we are still descended from Adam, the first Adam, with whom we share the fact that we will die. Spiritually, however, we can all be wrested from death by Christ, the Christ who, as the "last Adam," became a life-giving spirit. By awaking the original, heavenly physical human being, Christ bestows a new form of heredity on us. He enables us to share in a heavenly body that is imperishable, spiritual, immortal, and not subject to earthly corruption.

In this pure figure, consisting of divine formative forces, Mary Magdalene saw Christ on Easter morning near the empty tomb, and she did not recognize him. Until he spoke to her, she was unaware of who stood before her. On the first day of his resurrection, the risen Lord also walked to Emmaus with two men from the larger circle of disciples; they, too, were unable to recognize who accompanied them. After they recognized him that evening at an inn in Emmaus, he appeared that evening in the circle of the close disciples in Jerusalem. Luke and John relate, respectively in their chapters 24 and 20, how hesitant the disciples were to accept that it was the Christ.

Evidently, they all found it hard to take the step from the Jesus they followed in Palestine to the Christ. What now stood before them was the transformed human being, who in his corporeality no longer dragged death along with him. The restored physical body, however, was invisible. What they perceived was the etheric body, the suprasensory body that, at moments of great inner power, can become visible. Christ appeared to them in that body, and in this sense we might recall the second suprasensory world that is perceptible in our world but is usually not recognized (as described in chapter 7). Through the power of his etheric body, the entire physical body of Christ was able to appear to those who had an inner connection with him.

Spiritually, we have all been wrested from death by Christ, and with our material body we continue to return to the Earth from which it was taken, but now not entirely as dust. Today we inhabit our physical and etheric bodies far more intensely than people did in ancient times; we completely submerge ourselves in them and identify with them. This leaves traces, because when we die we leave a body behind in which a human soul and spirit have lived intensely, a body that has known the human form. Consequently, the dust that returns to dust in the Earth through cremation or burial is changed somewhat. It "ferments" the Earth and helps it stay together; it is prevented from being scattered to the four winds. Thus the spiritual decay of Earth is counteracted, which would have taken place a long time ago without the continued addition of such fermentation. Without the formative forces of human bodies, the Earth would have long ago become uninhabitable for humanity.

Appendix 3: Developmental Stages of Universe and Earth

(See chapter 3)

In his book *An Outline of Esoteric Science,* Rudolf Steiner describes how the question of human origins leads, through spiritual–scientific research, to the beginning of planet Earth and the time when all material existence began, and before which only spiritual reality existed. If we follow the process of how matter manifested, we see how spiritual reality originally "condensed" into material existence. Prior conditions of the Earth will then appear to spiritual powers of observation.

Thus we develop the insight that our Earth is the re-embodiment of an ancient heavenly body that itself went through three preceding planetary conditions. These are separated by conditions in a purely spiritual state, in which all that had become "physical" is reabsorbed into a spiritual mode of existence. The word *physical* indicates laws that can appear, for instance, in a variety of so-called aggregations of earthly materiality, as well as in various kinds of ether. It is thus an inner law that can be expressed in numerous manifestations. Preceding forms of the Earth's development are still present and distinguishable alongside its current forms of existence, said Steiner.*

The three preceding incarnations of the Earth are called Ancient Saturn, Ancient Sun, and Ancient Moon. These terms indicate that the dimensions of our present Earth during those incarnations were equal to the cosmic space within

* Rudolf Steiner, *An Outline of Esoteric Science,* pp. 130ff.

the current orbits of the planets. In their sequence to our present Earth, we can also see how materiality was gradually concentrated. Steiner emphasized with extensive descriptions, however, that it is difficult to form a picture of evolutionary processes in such a distant past with our current concepts and images.

Developments that lead to planetary incarnations are all carried by spiritual beings and their activities. All developments are those of spiritual beings; they come to expression through processes. Various groups of spiritual beings might work together; they also frequently work in succession, and we are able to recognize different stages in those processes. Like human beings, in the beginning of their development such beings depend on other beings. The purpose of development is to grow beyond those stages of dependence, progressing from taking to giving.

All development moves forward because of beings who learned to give. The plans behind all cosmic development spring from the Trinity. During successive stages of evolution, beings of the various spiritual realms reach comparable levels of development, but this does not suggest that evolution itself does not progress, as well. We never find simple repetitions of previous stages of development in the universe.

These spiritual beings (the angels of the nine heavenly hierarchies) were outlined in connection with the details of their cosmic tasks at the end of chapter 6.

Phases of Development

The shortest of such phases of development are time periods that we can still grasp historically, referred to as "cultural epochs." Each lasts about 2,160 years, during which we generally experience two incarnations (as described in chapter 11). There are seven such cultural epochs in an era. We live in the fifth of seven post-Atlantean cultural epochs. In addition to the preceding Atlantean, Lemurian, and two earlier epochs, as well as two to come, the current post-Atlantean epoch forms a cohesive stage of development; each such stage forms one of the seven incarnations of planetary evolution. At the end of its evolution, our Earth will have had seven such incarnations, beginning with Ancient Saturn.

Just as human beings enter a period of suprasensory existence after death to prepare for the next physical incarnation, something analogous happens to the Earth. Between its incarnations it passes through periods of rest, during which it exists in a state of spiritualization.

Our Own Situation

At the present time, the Earth has had three planetary incarnations, each with seven evolutionary epochs, and is now in the fourth round of the "earthly" phases, its fourth incarnation, called Earth. We find ourselves therefore past the midpoint of the overall evolution of our planet.

All of this offers a dazzling perspective that nonetheless becomes a little less overwhelming when we remember that a development expressed in numbers does not proceed in a linear way. In the cycles of its incarnations, the planet passes through rhythmic "breathing" phases of physical contraction and expansion. In this sense, we should bear in mind that the word *physical* indicates laws that can appear in various different conditions. At our stage in the development of Earth, *physical* coincides with matter. However, we have already gone past the time when we, as humankind, could have developed in

Sketch of cosmic evolution as described by Rudolf Steiner

the right way by refining our physical forces. Among the forces currently present and at work in the Earth, purely spiritual forces are becoming increasingly important. In this rhythmic becoming, we are reminded of what we ourselves go through in Sun existence, after death, during the periods of rhythmic breathing in and breathing out, rhythmic periods of social existence and inner solitude (see chapter 8).

As human beings, we are always an integral part of these developments; during the preceding incarnations of Earth, the seeds of our current three bodies were planted—the physical, etheric, and astral bodies. The seed for the "I" is laid during the current, earthly phase, and during the next three incarnations of this planet it is the intention that our present three corporeal bodies will be transformed into spiritual bodies. This is the task of the "I," with its three soul capacities of thinking, feeling, and the will that live in the soul. The three members of the soul—the sentient soul, intellectual soul, and consciousness soul—form part of a gradually developing individuality.

The development indicated here forms the background to what was said in chapter 2 about faith, love, and hope, the forces that help the soul find its way into its own world after death.

Appendix 4: Coming Back Soon?

(*See chapter 7*)

Thinking about reincarnation, and even the experience of it, has become increasingly common in the past few decades. It is noteworthy that Rudolf Steiner said in 1919 that it was high time for people to develop new relationships with one another based on the facts of reincarnation.* At the end of my conclusion to this book, I quoted Steiner's statement—that it will become an actual defect in our soul constitution if we are unable to recognize in others what is present in their souls from the previous life. Of course, it is a singular capacity for a person to be able to interact in this way with others. Nonetheless, the prerequisite for this—namely, the concept of reincarnation—is becoming a matter of fact for more and more people. Those who base their whole worldview on the Bible and cannot find reincarnation there and consequently reject it are now in the minority.**

Today we also hear of many people who have dramatic memories of a prior life—or, at least, believe that some of those memories are from a prior life. Especially shocking and moving are the "impossible" memories of those in whom a Jewish life rises that was ended by the systematic persecution by the Nazis.

Yonassan Gershom, an American rabbi in the East-European Hassidic tradition, describes people who are convinced

---

* Rudolf Steiner, *Understanding Society through Spiritual–Scientific Knowledge*, Sept. 12, 1919.

** In this regard see, for example, Edward Reaugh Smith, *The Soul's Long Journey: How the Bible Reveals Reincarnation;* also, Rudolf Frieling, *Christianity and Reincarnation.*

they perished in the Holocaust. In two books he documents how people deal with the terror that rises in them when they realize that it is connected with a prior life forcing its way into their consciousness—often the life of a child or young person brought to an early end in this way.* These are mostly individuals who reincarnated within a decade after the end of World War II. Gershom describes how he always hesitates to accept stories related to reincarnation images and keeps a list of criteria to evaluate them. He is familiar with the phenomenon of appropriating memories of others and experiencing them as one's own. He is also familiar with the idea of two "coming and going souls" who have intense interaction just before birth and immediately after death. The result is that such incarnating souls may take into life, as their own memories, the memories of those who just died.

It is a story in itself how Gershom gives the idea of reincarnation (which is completely foreign to traditional Judaism) a place in the mysticism of the Jewish soul. This soul, he says, once it has made its covenant with its God, will always remain Jewish. In this way, he helps many people come to terms with the pictures that they carry in them.

I must also mention Barbro Karlén, who writes of her conviction that she is the reincarnation of Anne Frank.** She understands the abuse, torment, and persecution heaped upon her when she makes a connection with what Anne Frank suffered in her captivity. What she experiences in this way is a kind of recapitulation of the experiences she ascribes to Anne Frank.

---

* Yonassan Gershom, *Beyond the Ashes: Cases of Reincarnation from the Holocaust;* and *From Ashes to Healing: Mystical Encounters with the Holocaust: Fifteen True Stories.*

** Barbro Karlén, *And the Wolves Howled: Fragments of Two Lifetimes.*

Whose Past?

This is a fundamental motif that we encounter in such descriptions—that the current life is experienced as an immediate continuation of the previous one. The outer circumstances differ, but inwardly one carries the baggage one has been unable to process properly. We should certainly question such interpretations.

A typical aspect of kamaloka (the period that soon follows death) is detachment, leaving the body behind as the necessary element for the ability to feel and will and as a means of thinking. With the integration of the loosening etheric body into the etheric world, the relief of dying consists of the fact that the angels of the third heavenly hierarchy receive our web of destiny. Consequently, we are not left on our own to process and work through our experiences in the life just ended.

Rudolf Steiner mentioned that human beings can return quickly—much too quickly. As examples of exceptions to the general rule of two incarnations in each cultural epoch, he spoke about criminals who lead irresponsible lives and look out only for "number one." There are also people who, like the seventeenth-century English politician Oliver Cromwell, crave power and are unable to move away from the Earth.

Is it necessary or justified to seize on the idea of reincarnation when shreds of memories waft through people? Or is this idea merely a band-aid, a convenient notion in such cases, because so many people seem to subscribe to it? Are we to believe the point of view of the industry that delves into such memories and has joined the ranks of service professions—that we are always dealing with personal memories of the persons involved?

We have seen that in our life between death and a new birth there are moments when there is a distinct connection with life on Earth. There is the moment in Sun existence during the descent when we have a lively connection with the Earth and what is going on there. In Rudolf Steiner's example, we have such a connection some four hundred years before our next incarnation, when we look down upon our line of future ancestors, at the end of which are our future parents. Such impressions can be so strong that they evoke a kind of déja vu. This phenomenon indicates that, out of the spiritual world, it is possible to have a strong identification with what is happening on the Earth, but of course it says nothing about whether we return slowly or quickly.

Strong impressions might also come to meet us just before birth, when we meet those who have just died and bring with them in their souls all that they experienced in their life on Earth. This is an important moment; in such an encounter we get an impression of what awaits us. In lectures in 1919, Rudolf Steiner pointed out that, "for the past seven to ten years," children were born with a remarkable expression on their faces. It's as if they exhibit a kind of dull somberness and reluctance, as if they really didn't want to come to the Earth. Steiner blamed such a melancholic expression on the fact that, in their encounters just before birth, they were confronted with the materialistic attitudes awaiting them on Earth. They knew that their souls' wings would be "clipped."*

This makes clear the real effects of what people take into the suprasensory world from their life on Earth. All of this becomes an important experience for those who are about to

* Rudolf Steiner, *Understanding Society through Spiritual–Scientific Knowledge*, June 12, 1919.

be born; it helps them orient themselves and prepares them for the coming life.*

People who were able to prepare adequately for death will bring with them a ferment of processing in their soul; they will have already begun to detach themselves from the Earth. This was different, however, for the children and adults who were murdered in the concentration camps. Their shocking and overwhelming experiences will go with them, largely unprocessed, into the spiritual world. Initially, those experiences lead an independent life and pervade, with all their horrors, the spiritual sphere in which other souls are preparing for a new birth.

General Spiritual Realities

There are still a few things of a more general nature that are important in this context. One phenomenon was mentioned in chapter 11. Part of the destiny that is awaiting us is the metamorphosis the angels of the first hierarchy have made of what human beings went through together on Earth. Some thirty to fifty years later this rains down into the souls of then-living human beings.**

Is this the background behind the remarkable phenomenon that the Holocaust was suddenly no longer hushed up the way it was in the first decades after World War II? And also the fact that around the same time a militant neo-Nazism reared its head in which really the specters of the past go round, manipulated by the power that aims to kill all spirituality?

Here we also have to mention the aspect that has to do with the "vertical migration" currently taking place. When he used

* Rudolf Steiner, *Vergangenheits- und Zukunftsimpule im sozialen Geschehen*, Mar. 23, 1919.

** Rudolf Steiner, *Karmic Relationships*, vol. 3, July 4, 1924.

this term, Rudolf Steiner reminded us that in former times spiritual life was tied to the blood. When we wanted to reappear on Earth we chose a body from the race and people that offered us the best opportunities. Bound to a specific part of the Earth's surface, such a race and people provided us with the factors of heredity that we needed. Since the beginning of modern times, this has begun to change; race and people are no longer so important as they once were. According to Steiner, souls who want to incarnate direct themselves increasingly toward geographical circumstances. Europeans, North Americans, and Asians, especially, choose where they want to incarnate, perhaps in mountains rather than in plains or a particular climate; they don't consider race or ethnicity. In addition to vertical migration, there is the soul migration from West to East (mentioned in chapter 11).

The vertical migration is also expressed in a spiritual sense. At one time, Christianity coming from the Southeast was met by barbaric hordes that invaded Europe from the East to the Southwest. What we know as Europe today arose as a cultural and spiritual reality in these encounters. Today, waves of spiritual activity are entering our world, and it is important to meet these with a disposition receptive to the spirit.*

We also have to consider a more personal aspect. People who think they are communicating with a deceased person might instead be contacting the etheric body the deceased person has left behind in the elemental world. Under certain circumstances, an etheric body can pose as a real individuality living in the spiritual world.**

* Rudolf Steiner, *Vergangenheits- und Zukunftsimpulse im sozialen Geschehen*, Apr. 13, 1919; also *Problems of Society*, Sept. 13, 1919.

** Rudolf Steiner, *Understanding Society through Spiritual–Scientific Knowledge*, Feb. 6, 1917.

Sources of Misunderstandings

We are witnessing today a resurgence of the old inclinations toward mediumship, though now in the form that we can all become our own medium. Plunge into yourself, into your memories; discover yourself in your prior lives, and you can heal many of your problems! Perhaps—but the solace that people find when they plunge into such memories usually does not go beyond the psychological level, where we talk ourselves out of things that oppress us. The conclusion that such torments arise from a prior life is certainly debatable. It is especially in this area, when we plunge into ourselves and encounter inner images, that we can also encounter surprises. The following example might suffice; it is instructive and indicates how we can be fooled by pictures that are derived in some way from our own inner being.

In lectures given in 1913, Rudolf Steiner discussed at length the so-called Paradise imagination—wonderful pictures of Paradise that live in our imagination.* Such pictures might arise in us when we suddenly become clairvoyant during sleep. In what is displayed before our inner eye, however, we are not looking back at the ancient Garden of Eden. These pictures arise directly from our own bodily constitution; Paradise, infinitely multiplied, continues to be present in everyone's organs—in our nervous system, metabolism, and blood circulation. There is no question, therefore, of an objective spiritual reality outside us. Thus there is every reason to doubt interpretations based on the assumption that reincarnation pictures are objective remnants of our personal prior life. This is what Irene Diet characterized as "reincarnation bereft of spirit,"** a direct consequence

* Rudolf Steiner, *The Effects of Esoteric Development*, Mar. 25 and 28, 1913.

** Irene Diet, "Die entgeistigte Wiederverkörperung," in *Das Goetheanum*, Oct. 17, 1999.

of modern materialism that has found its way into ideas of reincarnation and karma.

The Will to Return Quickly

During the final few months of his public activities, Rudolf Steiner spoke of people who want to return quickly.* He spoke about his listeners who were able to take Anthroposophy into themselves with true, heartfelt devotion. He predicted that they would *want* to come back at the end of the twentieth century. Along with others who were not recently incarnated, they would want to help strengthen spirituality on Earth for the sake of saving our human culture.

It seems to me that, with such people, we can see a somewhat longer period between incarnations than for those living with nightmares of the Holocaust. The reason behind coming back quickly is completely different. Regarding the people Steiner spoke about, it is not a matter of being stuck in the remnants of a previous incarnation. This is not the mood described by the author of the Book of Revelation concerning the souls hiding under the heavenly altar because they have not come to terms with death and are not yet wearing their "white robes" (Rev. 6:9–11). In Steiner's description of those who would want to be present again at the end of the twentieth century, we become aware of the activity of souls who have left the protection of the heavenly altar in their white robes. They are capable of contributing to the progress in the heavens that was set in motion by the sacrifice of the Lamb (Rev. 7:9–17).

* Rudolf Steiner, *Karmic Relationships*, vol. 3.

Appendix 5: Suicide

(*See chapter 9*)

When Rudolf Steiner spoke in 1914 about the unused forces that people who die young have available to them in the life that precedes the next birth, he emphasized that this is not true for people who take their own life. To the extent explanations were necessary, he described the consequences of an artificially induced early death in his book *Theosophy*. He pointed out that suicides have to go through the experiences of the fourth soul region, that of pleasure and displeasure, very intensely. This is the region where we have to surmount the longing for the body with which we identified on Earth (see chapter 2).

In the case of suicide, feelings of identification with the body are unable to die off gradually, as it happens after a natural death. This is why one who commits suicide feels suddenly "hollowed out"; there is nothing left to take hold of the powerful sense of self. After such a death, the illusion of the physical persists in the soul just as strongly as it did during life on Earth.*

When Rudolf Steiner mentioned suicide in subsequent lectures he returned to these aspects repeatedly. If we have strongly identified with our physical existence—the "I" with our body—a strong desire for that body arises after death. We feel like a hollowed-out tree, as if we had lost our "I." We continuously thirst for our self.

* Rudolf Steiner, *The Inner Nature of Man,* Apr. 14, 1914.

Don't forget; *everyone* faces a tremendous emptiness after death, and we have to reorient ourselves and rediscover our feeling of self. In the case of a suicide, however, the feeling of emptiness is so strong because the astral body was unprepared for the fact that it has to continue without the physical body. When the unity of the physical, etheric, and astral bodies is broken, the suicide then lacks a physical body; he or she feels as if hollowed out and sets out in great pain on a desperate search for that lost body. Those who leave the body in this unnatural way go into death without having had one particular and essential experience. Such persons have to live on without ever having had the complete experience of the physical body, because that is possible only at the moment of dying. This experience allows us to look back at the moment of dying throughout our existence between death and rebirth, and this reawakens our feeling of self each time.*

Without this experience human beings also miss an important encounter. Around the middle of life, between our twenty-eighth and forty-second years, in the depths of our soul we all encounter the divine being who carries the world, God the Father. People who die younger have this meeting at the moment of death, provided death is not self-inflicted. If we take our own life, we avoid that meeting, since suicide robs us of the possibility of experiencing ourselves as a reality in the context of the world in which we live.

The Hollow of the "I"

Rudolf Steiner gives the distressing picture of the hollowed-out tree, the experience of the suicide of feeling

* Rudolf Steiner, *Der Mensch in Zusammenhang mit dem Kosmos 9*, Dec. 7, 1921.

hollowed-out. He emphasizes that, if we knew what awaits us, we would never take our own life. This picture is so distressing because it directly involves what we call our "I." We recall the fact that our real "I" always remains behind at birth and is not born on Earth. What we call our "I," the entity through which we experience our self, is only a reflection within the body of our true "I." As we have seen, we are aware of it only in between our experiences, in the gaps in our consciousness, in its hollows. If this were not so, we would never be able to make a bridge to other human beings, because we would always push ourselves into the foreground. The phenomenon that we observe our "I" *between our experiences* is shown in the alternation of waking and sleeping.

Consciously, we know nothing of what happens when we are sleeping, and we accept matter-of-factly the gaps that sleep causes in the continuity of our consciousness. But, it is precisely in those gaps during sleep that communication with the true "I" takes place and where the beginning of destiny starts to form.

When we are not asleep, however, there is more than just these gaps in consciousness. We cannot look for our "I" within ourselves but have to look for it in the outer world. It is a remarkable fact that every human being we meet and with whom we have some interaction has more of a relationship to our "I" than we do ourselves. We live in a social era in which we have to say: *My being is with all those whom I meet out in the world. It is there that I meet myself, not when I plunge into myself.* We discover a modern experience of the injunction "Know yourself," which was written on the temple of Apollo in Delphi. It is through our contact with others that we get a hint of our true "I." Thus the hollow created in me through the absence of my "I" is filled by the influence of other human beings.*

Rudolf Steiner once used a wonderful image when he spoke of the Nordic folk tale, *The Dream Song of Olaf Åsteson,* "who lay so long a-sleeping."** He pointed out that we always have a hollow in our relationship to the spirit. If we want to create a relationship to the spiritual world as human beings, we have to go into the hollowness of it, as once happened to Moses, when he dedicated himself to the survival of the people God was going to abandon. The Old Testament uses an abundance of images for this (Ex. 33:12–23). People had always sensed that no one could see God and live. However, as God told Moses, we can stand in a "cave" and let the revealing power of the Godhead pass by. If we enter the cave, this power will cover us with His hand until we can see Him from behind. That's how it happened to Moses.

We find this hollow in ourselves, too. We experience our freedom in the hollow, the open space left in us by the true "I." This is our own, most personal hollow in which we can turn to the spirit. Here we become aware, indirectly, of what others bring to us, particularly in everything that plays a role in forming our destiny, and this is much more than we normally realize.***

Throughout our life we carry, in the hollow of our skull, a picture of the cave where Moses found protection. In this physical hollow, a special kind of thinking can manifest, thinking

* Rudolf Steiner, *How Can Mankind Find the Christ Again?* Dec. 27 and 28, 1918; also, "How Do I Find Christ?" (Oct. 16, 1918), included in Steiner, *Death as Metamorphosis of Life* (CW 182).

** See Rudolf Steiner, *Our Connection with the Elemental World.*

*** Rudolf Steiner, *Our Connection with the Elemental World*, Dec. 31, 1914.

that is not analytical and does not "divide and conquer," but thinking that connects and creates forms—what Rudolf Steiner called "Goethean thinking." It is the kind of thinking that can take in spiritual substance and work with it—the kind of thinking that leads directly to Christ.

Intimate Help

When we review these pictures of the hollowed-out human being, we may begin to suspect that a suicide brings with this deed a foreign element into the world of death. Usually, at death we connect ourselves with the true "I," which during life can manifest itself only in the hollow; we enter the hollow, so to say.

Behind suicide stands not only the person's overburdened identification with physical existence, because of which the experience of the senselessness of this existence has become too strong. A most important factor in cases of suicide seems to be that these human beings must not have had the capacity to meet themselves sufficiently in other people. Their own hollow was insufficiently filled. And for that reason, they take the hollow (which enables us on Earth to come into contact with ourselves) with them into death, and they are condemned to lose themselves in it.

In *Light beyond Darkness,* Doré Deverell describes her experiences with "the healing of a suicide," her son. She shows how, through Anthroposophy, she learned to read to the dead and to use meditative verses. She could sense that he found peace. It seems, by offering the help that anyone can give to the dead, that she created a human atmosphere in which her son was able to find sufficient support, support that he had not been able to find during his life.

The meditative verses that Rudolf Steiner gave especially to people who wanted to help someone after a suicide speak for themselves.

The following is a good example:

Your will was weak.
Make your will strong.
I send you warmth for your coldness.
I send you light for your darkness.
I send you my love.
I am sending you my thought.
Continue to develop.*

The next two verses were given to a mother who lost her husband at a young age. The son had to manage without his father, which may have been a motive for his suicide. The first verse is addressed to the son; the second to the husband.

Soul in the land of souls,
seek the grace of Christ,
the grace that brings you help,
help from the lands of spirit,
which also grants inner rest
to spirits who would despair
in restless experience.

You, companion of my life,
help our offspring;
my thoughts go out to you,
to bring them in the right way
to him, I ask your soul,
my husband.

These two verses indicate how much someone who committed suicide needs help, to the point that a deceased soul who was deeply connected with this person is evoked in order to help him. People who take their own life have to forego both experiences that are connected with the moment of dying. The living can try, at least, in a human way to help them find their way in their new life.

---

* Franz Gerner, a painter, requested this verse for a person who had taken his own life a few years before World War I (unpublished).

Appendix 6: Necessary Evil

(See the Conclusion)

For ancient peoples, the battle between light and darkness, good and evil, was a cosmic process of which they were part. People could become the instrument of good powers or evil powers. They could also become the victim of those powers, as in the story of Job. But for Job, a personal moral disposition breaks through and helps that human individual take responsibility for his relationship to good and evil. We know, then, that we human beings are more than nature and are morally responsible for our actions; we can be guilty in relation to our fellow human beings and to God.

When people in ancient times encountered evil as a cosmic principle, they also knew that it had become evil only through the course of evolution. Evil occurs when a cosmic principle maintains its original actions into later times, isolating itself and deserting evolutionary progress. Evil is actually goodness that has fallen behind, that wants to perpetuate itself into the present. We can understand from this that if evil has actually become evil by manifesting at the wrong time then absolute evil cannot exist.

As always in the cosmos, it is a matter of spiritual beings in what we human beings recognize as a process, or principle. There are, for example, spiritual beings whose goal is to retard evolution. They oppose those spiritual beings who wish to promote evolution. Only through such battles does the good truly last; thus evolution also becomes progress. The memory of such confrontations in a cosmic past is preserved in images such as the battle of Michael against the dragon (Rev. 12), as a result of which heavenly bodies have even come into being.

Those who can see behind the scenes, as Rudolf Steiner did, can discover that the beings who fall behind use the opportunities offered by the higher spiritual powers who serve progress.* In the process, an opening to freedom is created, and with freedom, in turn, comes responsibility. We get an impression of this reality in the story of Abraham, who was asked to sacrifice his own son to his God. In the end, Abraham's sacrifice was unnecessary in a physical sense because God accepted his inner sacrifice as real.

"Giving someone the opportunity" and thereby giving an opponent the chance to do what he wants to do—in service of a higher objective—was manifested in the way Jesus Christ accepted Judas Iscariot into his circle of disciples, and thereby consciously accepted the role Judas would play through treason.

Lucifer and Ahriman

This space for freedom was implanted by the luciferic powers into our developing "I"-consciousness. One human being could thus separate from another, and also develop the ability to create sufficient distance between their self and the outer world so that it truly became a sensory outer world. In this world, ahrimanic beings have their chance to delude people into thinking that our everyday world is the only real world.

Lucifer is the power that wants to "preserve" the eternal, which constantly moves and changes in the spiritual world, and wants to make it sustainable through time. He wants to make it a "snapshot," something gripped in the moment

* Rudolf Steiner, *Inner Experiences of Evolution.*

that is individual and will develop as such. He wants to bring all the treasures, all the essence of the suprasensory, into the sensory so it becomes a reflection, a revelation of it. He wants to bring everything that is not yet openly known into the light—into *his* light.

Lucifer is the being who stands behind the rise of the individual, with all its good as well as objectionable sides. Without a whiff of selfishness, human beings could not be creative artists, but if their egoism wants to serve only themselves they become isolated and hardened in themselves. Whoever would avoid Lucifer because of the dangers he creates for people on Earth would just as well have to avoid fire—for we could burn ourselves by fire. But whoever purges the very last dregs of egoism within will find a good leader in Lucifer.

Ahriman hopes to lift everything that has value in the sensory world into eternity. He wants everything sensory, into which he has nestled, to become eternal. He wants no metamorphosis, no change; for him there are no preparatory or preliminary stages; everything must remain as it is. Nothing must be lost; nothing is transient to him.

We can recognize Ahriman's intentions in our temptation to hold on to what we consider personally valuable. In actual life, however, we have to learn to sift through things, we have to learn discernment and to let go.

These two powers, therefore, do not merely appear at the wrong time; they also want to perpetuate, each in their own way. We saw that Lucifer wants to freeze the spiritual within a material mode of existence. But, without the influence of Lucifer, for instance, we would be invisible on Earth; our body would not have developed a strong affinity to products that decay and eventually perish. If the spiritual were imprisoned in matter, all that lives would lose its divine component. Only death rescues all that lives from the fate of becoming completely and forever earthly.

The story of Paradise, with its warning *"You shall die"* (Gen. 2:17), preserves the memory of the gift of death, without which we would be totally surrendered to the obstructing powers and would become completely estranged from our spiritual home. Without Christ, our dying would have become a terminus, the final station of a long journey, with no prospect of continued existence. Christ's victory over death has made possible life in death, life that opens the door to the heavenly worlds. The two forms in which evil acts in our world are described in detail in Hans-Werner Schroeder's book *Necessary Evil.*

The Center between the Two

If we want an image of the relationship of people to the two forms of evil, then we need a trinity, the image of three that is the primordial image of everything that is becoming. Confusion arises where a black-and-white mindset wants to live only in opposites, such as heaven and hell, good and evil, or body and soul.

In the existent, revealed world, we can think in terms of duality. In the world that is still in the making, we touch reality only with the idea of trinity. Then we see the divine standing in the middle, creating a balance between the ahrimanic extreme on the one hand and the luciferic extreme on the other. We see in Christ the one who always knows the balance between the two.

Thus we can find the "modern trinity," in the words of Rudolf Steiner, with the human being in the center, who has to create his own equilibrium between the ahrimanic and luciferic extremes.* We always have to find the midpoint, the precise balance between the two extremes of which we can become victims. Finding the balance between the two extremes is a basic Christian task.

Rudolf Steiner wanted to represent this in a great statue, carved from wood, of Christ between Lucifer and Ahriman. The unfinished sculpture was saved from the fire that destroyed the first Goetheanum because it had been in a workshop nearby. About four years after the six-foot-high model of the sculpture was completed, Rudolf Steiner said that it was intended as one great countenance, all physiognomy, with the power and mobility of expression we otherwise find only in the human face.**

Such an image can help strengthen the mutual understanding between beings who exist only as soul and spirit and beings who are also physically embodied. Christ is shown between Lucifer and Ahriman. Christ is vanquishing Ahriman at his feet and overcoming Lucifer above, who wants to transport the human being to dizzying heights. In the center, Christ appears in this modern trinity as the "Representative of Humanity" between the two spiritual opposing powers.

For us human beings, repeatedly finding the middle is a creative inner act in daily life. Those who seek physical matter and material affairs in the outer world interpret the world in keeping with Ahriman; those who seek abstract truths within their being are acting in the way of Lucifer. The point is never to make sharp distinctions between inner and outer, always

* Rudolf Steiner, *Conscious Society*, pp. 128–129.

** Rudolf Steiner, *Vergangenheits- und Zukunftsimpulse im sozialen Geschehen*, Mar. 30, 1919.

"The Representative of Humanity" by Rudolf Steiner

trying instead to connect the two. As human beings, we always have to renew and reestablish such moments of balance, since we always tend toward one of the two extremes. We especially need to maintain a balance between everything that might carry us away into fanaticism or mysticism, on the one hand, and on the other, what might make us identify exclusively with the Earth. The third part of the equation has its place between these extremes. We are that third part.

Luciferic beings would like to see the world, especially human beings, abandon the divine creative powers and instead become unfaithful to them. Ahrimanic beings want primarily to bring all humanity, along with the whole Earth, into their sphere of influence and make everything dependent on them.

In Life and Death

Let's recall a statement in the Conclusion—that when children and young people die, they bring a certain "weight" into the spiritual world that would otherwise be missing, and that as we grow older, we emanate spiritual substance into the earthly world. When Rudolf Steiner remarked on this, he went on to say that when children and young people add this weight to the spiritual world as they die they prevent the luciferic powers from completely separating the spiritual world from the physical world. Aging people who emanate spiritual substance on Earth help to thwart Ahriman's intentions; because of them, spirit remains present on Earth.

In our existence between death and the next birth, creative divine beings make extensive use of both luciferic and ahrimanic powers. Without the help of the ahrimanic powers, our upper pole—that monument of our past—would not receive the human form. We do not go around with a head that expresses our character directly. The human head has a stronger form than we encounter in, for example, a bull or a lamb. We owe that new, hardened human head—the continuity with our past—to the ahrimanic powers.

Without the luciferic powers, our lower pole could not be transformed and prepared for the next incarnation. Lucifer assists creative spirits to maintain the human form. During the second stage of existence between death and our next birth, Ahriman then helps to put the human stamp on our coming physiognomy. In our incarnation between death and the coming birth, luciferic and ahrimanic powers assist us in this way.

Cited and Related Works

Anonymous. *The Bridge over the River: After Death Communications of a Young Artist Who Died in World War I.* SteinerBooks, 1974.

Archiati, Pietro. *Reincarnation in Modern Life: Towards a New Christian Awareness.* Temple Lodge, 1998.

Benesch, Friedrich. *Apocalypse, the Transformation of Earth: An Esoteric Mineralogy.* Lindisfarne Books, 2015.

Blatchford, Claire. *Experiences with the Dying and the Dead: Waking to Our Connections with Those Who Have Died.* Lindisfarne Press, 2007.

Blattmann, Georg. *The Sun: The Ancient Mysteries and the New Physics.* Floris Books, 1985.

Bock, Emil. *The Rhythm of the Christian Year.* Floris Books, 1992.

Bockemühl, Almut. *The Twilight Years: Thoughts on Old Age, Death, and Dying.* Temple Lodge, 2015.

Boogert, Arie. *What Happens after We Die: Making the Connection between the Living and the Dead.* Lindisfarne Books, 2021.

Deverell, Doré. *Light beyond Darkness: The Healing of a Suicide across the Threshold of Death.* Clairview. 2000.

Frieling, Rudolf. *Christianity and Reincarnation.* Floris Books, 2015.

———. *Hidden Treasures in the Psalms* (3rd ed.). Floris Books, 2015.

Gershom, Yonassan. *Beyond the Ashes: Cases of Reincarnation from the Holocaust.* Are Press, 1992.

———. *From Ashes to Healing: Mystical Encounters with the Holocaust: Fifteen True Stories.* Are Press, 1996.

Harwood, A. C. (ed.). *The Faithful Thinker,* Hodder & Stoughton, 1961.

Jocelyn, Beredene. *Citizens of the Cosmos: Life's Unfolding from Conception through Death to Rebirth.* SteinerBooks, 2009.

Karlén, Barbro. *And the Wolves Howled. Fragments of Two Lifetimes.* Clairview Books, 2000.

Lusseyran, Jacques. *And There Was Light: Autobiography of Jacques Lusseyran: Blind Hero of the French Resistance.* Morning Light, 2006.

Madsen, Jon. *The New Testament: A Rendering*. Floris Books, 1994.

Mees, L.F.C. *Secrets of the Skeleton: Form in Metamorphosis*. SteinerBooks, 2005.

Miller, Sukie. *After Death: Mapping the Journey*. Simon & Schuster, 1997.

Morgenstern, Christian. *We Have Found a Path*. Mercury Press, 2013.

Porphyry. *On the Cave of the Nymphs* (trans. by Thomas Taylor). Phanes, 1991.

Prokofieff, Sergei O. *And the Earth Becomes a Sun: The Mystery of the Resurrection*. Wynstones Press, 2015.

Rittelmeyer, Friedrich. *Reincarnation: A Christian Perspective* (3rd ed.), Floris Books, 2018.

Rozell, Calvert. *The Near-death Experience: In the Light of Scientific Research and Rudolf Steiner's Spiritual Science,* 2nd ed. Lindisfarne Books, 2018.

Schroeder, Hans-Werner. *Necessary Evil: Origin and Purpose*. Floris Books, 2005.

Selg, Peter. *The Path of the Soul after Death: The Community of the Living and the Dead as Witnessed by Rudolf Steiner in his Eulogies and Farewell Addresses*. SteinerBooks, 2010.

———. *Unbornness: Human Pre-existence and the Journey toward Birth*. SteinerBooks, 2010.

Shepherd, A. P. *Rudolf Steiner, Scientist of the Invisible: A Biography*. Inner Traditions, 1990.

Smith, Edward Reaugh. *The Soul's Long Journey: How the Bible Reveals Reincarnation*. SteinerBooks, 2003.

Stajano, Attilio. *Only Love Remains: Lessons from the Dying on the Meaning of Life: Euthanasia or Palliative Care?* Clairview, 2015.

Steffen, Albert. *Dreiunddreissig Jahre*. Verlag für schöne Wissenschaften, 1959.

Steiner, Rudolf. *According to Luke: The Gospel of Compassion and Love Revealed* (CW 114). SteinerBooks, 2001.

———. *According to Matthew: The Gospel of Christ's Humanity* (CW 123). SteinerBooks, 2002.

———. *Anthroposophical Leading Thoughts: Anthroposophy as a Path of Knowledge* (CW 26). Rudolf Steiner Press, 1973.

———. *The Apocalypse of St. John: Lectures on the Book of Revelation* (CW 104). Anthroposophic Press, 1985.

———. *Artistic Sensitivity as a Spiritual Approach to Knowing Life and the World* (CW 161). SteinerBooks, 2018.

———. *At Home in the Universe: Exploring Our Suprasensory Nature* (CW 231). Anthroposophic Press, 2000.

———. *Building Stones for an Understanding of the Mystery of Golgotha: Human Life in a Cosmic Context* (CW 175). Rudolf Steiner Press, 2015.

———. *Chance, Providence, and Necessity* (CW 163). Anthroposophic Press, 1988.

———. *Concerning the Astral World and Devachan* (CW 88). SteinerBooks. 2018.

———. *The Connection between the Living and the Dead* (CW 168). SteinerBooks, 2017.

———. *Conscious Society: Anthroposophy and the Social Question* (CW 189). Rudolf Steiner Press, 2018.

———. *Cosmic and Human Metamorphosis*, 2nd ed. (CW 175). SteinerBooks, 2015.

———. *Cosmosophy, vol. 2: Cosmic Influences on the Human Being* (CW 208). Completion Press, 1997.

———. *Death as Metamorphosis of Life: Including "What Does the Angel Do in Our Astral Body?" and "How Do I Find Christ?"* (CW 182). SteinerBooks, 2008.

———. *Dying Earth and Living Cosmos: The Living Gifts of Anthroposophy—The Need for New Forms of Consciousness* (CW 181). Rudolf Steiner Press, 2015.

———. *The Effects of Esoteric Development* (CW 145). Anthroposophic Press, 1997.

———. *Eternal and Transient Elements in Human Life: The Cosmic Past of Humanity and the Mystery of Evil* (CW 184). SteinerBooks. 2016.

———. *From Jesus to Christ* (CW 131). Rudolf Steiner Press, 1991.

———. *From Limestone to Lucifer...: Answers to Questions* (CW 349). Rudolf Steiner Press, 1999.

———. *From the History and Contents of the First Section of the Esoteric School: Letters, Documents, and Lectures, 1904–1914* (CW 264). Anthroposophic Press, 2010.

———. *Das Geheimnis des Todes: Wesen und Bedeutung Mitteleuropas und die europäischen Volksgeister* (CW 159). Rudolf Steiner Verlag, 1967.

———. *Die geistigen Hintergründe des Ersten Weltkrieges: Kosmische und Menschliche Geschichte,* vol 7 (CW 174b). Rudolf Steiner Verlag, 1974.

———. *Der Goethanismus, ein Umwandlungsimpuls und Auferstehungsgedanke* (CW 188). Rudolf Steiner Verlag, 1982.

———. *How Can Mankind Find the Christ Again? The Threefold Shadow-Existence of Our Time and the New Light of Christ* (CW 187). Anthroposophic Press, 1984.

———. *The Healing Process: Spirit, Nature, and Our Bodies* (CW 319). SteinerBooks, 2010.

———. *How the Spiritual World Projects into Physical Existence: The Influence of the Dead* (CW 150). Rudolf Steiner Press, 2014.

———. *The Influence of the Dead on Destiny* (CW 179). SteinerBooks, 2007.

———. *Inner Experiences of Evolution* (CW 132). SteinerBooks, 2006.

———. *The Inner Nature of Man: And Our Life between Death and Rebirth* (CW 153). Rudolf Steiner Press, 2013.

———. *The Karma of Untruthfulness: Secret Societies, the Media, and Preparations for the Great War,* vol. 2 (CW 174). Rudolf Steiner Press, 2005.

———. *Karmic Relationships: Esoteric Studies,* 8 vols. (CW 236–9). Rudolf Steiner Press, 1955–2017.

———. *Human Evolution: A Spiritual–Scientific Quest* (CW 183). Rudolf Steiner Press, 2014.

———. *Life between Death and Rebirth: The Active Connection between the Living and the Dead* (CW 140). Anthroposophic Press, 1975.

———. *Life between Death and Rebirth in Relation to Cosmic Facts* (CW 141). Collison, 1930.

———. *Meditations for the Dead: Connecting to Those Who Have Died.* Rudolf Steiner Press, 2018.

———. *Der Mensch in Zusammenhang mit dem Kosmos 9: Nordische und mitteleuropäische Geistimpulse: Das Fest der Erscheinung Christi* (CW 209). Rudolf Steiner Verlag, 1968.

———. *Die Mission der neuen Geistesoffenbarung* (CW 127). Rudolf Steiner Verlag, 1911.

———. *The Mystery of the Trinity: Mission of the Spirit* (CW 214). SteinerBooks, 2016.

———. *Our Connection with the Elemental World: Kalevala–Olaf Åsteson–the Russian People: The World as the Result of Balancing Influences* (CW 158). Rudolf Steiner Press, 2017.

———. *Our Dead: Memorial, Funeral, and Cremation Addresses* (CW 261). SteinerBooks, 2011.

———. *An Outline of Esoteric Science* (CW 13). Anthroposophic Press, 1997.

———. *Prayers for Parents and Children* (from CW 40). Rudolf Steiner Press, 1995.

———. *The Presence of the Dead on the Spiritual Path* (CW 154). Anthroposophic Press, 1990.

———. *The Problems of Our Time.* Anthroposophic Press, n.d.

———. *Problems of Society: An Esoteric View, from Luciferic Past to Ahrimanic Future* (CW 193). Rudolf Steiner Press, 2016.

———. *Reincarnation and Karma: Two Fundamental Truths of Human Existence* (CW 135). SteinerBooks, 2001.

———. *Riddles of the Soul* (CW 21). Mercury Press, 1996.

———. *Rosicrucian Wisdom: An Introduction* (CW 99). Rudolf Steiner Press, 2000.

———. *Secrets of the Threshold* (CW 147). Anthroposophic Press, 1987.

———. *Die Soziale Grundforderung unserer Zeit* (CW 186). Rudolf Steiner Verlag, 1990.

———. *Spirit as Sculptor of the Human Organism: The Influence of the Dead* (CW 218). Rudolf Steiner Press, 2014.

———. *Spiritual Beings in the Heavenly Bodies and in the Kingdoms of Nature* (CW 136). SteinerBooks. 2011.

———. *Spiritual Science as a Foundation for Social Forms* (CW 199). Anthroposophic Press, 1986.

———. *Staying Connected: How to Continue Your Relationships with Those Who Have Died.* Anthroposophic Press, 1999.

———. *The Sun Mystery and the Mystery of Death and Resurrection: Exoteric and Esoteric Christianity* (CW 211). SteinerBooks, 2006.

———. *The Temple Legend: Freemasonry and Related Occult Movements: From the Contents of the Esoteric School* (cw 93). Rudolf Steiner Press, 2000.

———. *Theosophy: An Introduction to the Spiritual Processes in Human Life and in the Cosmos* (cw 9). Anthroposophic Press, 1994.

———. *True Knowledge of the Christ: Theosophy and Rosicrucianism* (cw 100). Rudolf Steiner Press, 2015.

———. *Truth-Wrought-Words: And Other Verses* (cw 40). Anthroposophic Press, 1979.

———. *Understanding Healing: Meditative Reflections on Deepening Medicine through Spiritual Science* (cw 316). Rudolf Steiner Press, 2013.

———. *Understanding Society through Spiritual–Scientific Knowledge: Social Threefolding, Christ, Lucifer, and Ahriman* (cw 191). Rudolf Steiner Press, 2017.

———. *Vergangenheits- und Zukunftsimpulse im sozialen Geschehen* (cw 190). Rudolf Steiner Verlag, 1980.

———. *Verses and Meditations.* Rudolf Steiner Press, 2004.

———. *A Way of Self-Knowledge: And the Threshold of the Spiritual World* (cw 16–17). SteinerBooks, 2006.

———. *A Western Approach to Reincarnation and Karma: Selected Lectures and Writings.* Anthroposophic Press, 1997.

———. *The World of the Senses and the World of the Spirit* (cw 134). Steiner Book Centre, 1979.

Tomberg, Valentin. *Christ and Sophia: Anthroposophic Meditations on the Old Testament, New Testament, and Apocalypse.* SteinerBooks, 2015.

Unger, Carl. *The Language of the Consciousness Soul: A Guide to Rudolf Steiner's "Leading Thoughts."* SteinerBooks, 2012.

———. *Steiner's Theosophy and Principles of Spiritual Science.* SteinerBooks, 2015.

van den Brink, Margarete, and Hans Stolp. *What Happens When We Die? Our Journey in the Afterlife.* Temple Lodge, 2017.

Wijnberg, Nicholas, and Philip Martyn. *Crossing the Threshold: Practical and Spiritual Guidance on Death and Dying, Based on the Work of Rudolf Steiner.* Temple Lodge, 2003.

Zeylmans, Renée. *Approaching Death: A Companion's Guide to the End of Life.* Floris Books, 2019.